UNHACKABLE HAPPINESS

The Ultimate Blueprint to Beat Burnout, Overcome Digital Anxiety, and Rewire Your Brain Using Modern Neuroscience and Ancient Wisdom

Hanika Deepchand

UNHACKABLE HAPPINESS

The Ultimate Blueprint to Beat Burnout, Overcome Digital Anxiety, and Rewire Your Brain Using Modern Neuroscience and Ancient Wisdom

- **Author:** Hanika Deepchand
- **Publisher:** Hima Deepchand Rajput
- **Country of Publication:** India
- **Contact Email:** contact.hanika15@gmail.com
- **ISBN:** 978-93-344-8199-0 (Paperback)

Prologue

When I initiated the drafting of this book, my baseline focus was anchored onto a solitary, unyielding objective—to rescue the contemporary human mind from the exhausting current of digital noise and return its long-lost emotional kingdom. Today, human beings subsist under a state of unseen servitude, where raw human attention is systematically harvested by technology cartels and human self-esteem is transactionalized across algorithmic social validation indices. Within modern enterprise landscapes, the hyper-glorified culture of hustle and the toxic vanity of perpetual busyness have locked our central nervous systems into a permanent state of being "Tired but Wired."

This prologue has been carefully curated from my personal investigations and lived reality. As both an independent publisher and author, I intend to establish an unyielding reassurance that this text does not represent a collection of generic theories. It functions as a precise, practical blueprint engineered to render your mind completely unhackable. As you move across these chapters, you will wake to the realization that tranquility is not a passing external variable waiting to be discovered, but an impregnable fort that already exists within your being.

—Hanika Deepchand

Acknowledgments

Navigating the immense creative trajectory required to lock the final parameters of this transformative book was a deeply profound journey. Today, with absolute mindfulness, I express profound appreciation to the forces that delivered the cognitive stamina to construct this unyielding framework.

Primary and unmatched, I bow before the infinite cosmic intelligence and the divine, which planted the foundational seed of this vision within my mind and guided my awareness. I extend my deep, unadulterated appreciation to my parents and family unit for their unyielding protection, their respect for my creative isolation, and their deep support which operated as my ultimate source of strength.

I archive my highest respect for the visionary neuroscientists, analytical psychologists, and ancient global seers whose profound maps of consciousness—specifically the *Shrimad Bhagavad Gita* and Stoic philosophy—granted the empirical scaffolding required to neutralize modern mental crises. Finally, to my valued readers, I express absolute gratitude; your unyielding determination to overthrow algorithmic manipulation and reclaim your cognitive freedom is the definitive victory of my labor. This book is sovereignly dedicated to your elevation.

—Hanika Deepchand

Preface

As a writer and deep behavioral researcher, when I observe the contemporary world, I register an unrelenting, systemic friction paralyzing human consciousness. Thirty-year-old professionals are falling casualty to clinical burnout cycles, spending critical currency navigating medical networks. Individuals lie paralyzed across late-night hours because their internal brain alarms and fear-detection circuits remain hyperactive 24/7, systematically blocking restorative sleep, while society at large collapses into unstructured anxieties and comparison traps. Bearing direct witness to this psychological decay ignited the internal birth of this workbook.

Behind the pages of this project lie years of dedicated investigation, personal reflection, and a steadfast refusal to yield to the constant digital noise that attempts to stall any creative human endeavor. My baseline focus was anchored onto a solitary, unyielding objective—to rescue the contemporary human mind from this exhausting current and return its long-lost emotional kingdom. Within modern enterprise landscapes, the hyper-glorified culture of hustle and the toxic vanity of perpetual busyness have locked our central nervous systems into a permanent state of being tired but wired. If we are to survive this unseen servitude, we must develop a strategic, rigorous, and highly structured approach to reclaim the throne of our focus.

Through this preface, I intend to establish absolute structural clarity: this manuscript contains zero superficial metaphors or speculative rhetoric. Every analytical case study archived across these chapters is anchored completely onto documented real-life occurrences. This workbook stands as a proprietary, customized mental operating manual designed to intercept automated algorithmic conditioning, halting you from existing as a fragile casualty of your environment and crowning you as the master sculptor of your own brain mass.

—Hanika Deepchand

Contents

PART 3
The Unhackable Protocols

Introduction

The New Immortality

Within the high-velocity, hyper-accelerated landscape of the 21st-century digital ecosystem, the definitive parameter of 'Immortality' has undergone a radical transformation. In classical historical eras, tracking immortality required an individual to carve their signature onto physical monuments or secure territorial dominance via military campaigns. However, across this modern hyper-connected matrix—where your raw human attention is continuously commodified every millisecond and software algorithms script your immediate mood—authentic immortality assumes a drastically distinct profile.

'The New Immortality' represents the sovereign biological capability to maintain your internal focus completely tranquil, self-regulated, and entirely Unhackable right at the center of an environment of chaotic noise.

The exact moment you protect your internal mental sovereignty from being compromised by 24/7 cognitive warfare, modern enterprise burnout, and systemic silent stress, you transcend the linear prison of industrial time. You cease to exist as a helpless digital product manipulated by a cursor on a monitor; you claim your absolute status as the immortal ruler of your own attention.

The contemporary human being exists in a state of physical continuity, yet their executive brain architecture is buried deep beneath the rubble of constant information overload. Their internal light has been entirely extinguished. This introduction operates as an absolute revolutionary declaration of independence from chemical and psychological servitude. By integrating the unyielding parameters of this blueprint, you hardwire an advanced state of Psychological Immunity that external metrics possess zero power to compromise.

To help you achieve this state, the architecture of this blueprint is structured into three distinct operational segments:

- **Part 1** ruthlessly decodes the precise neurological networks that digital systems seek to compromise and harvest.
- **Part 2** bridges advanced neuroplasticity frameworks directly with the unyielding, ancient blueprints of the Vedas, the Bhagavad Gita, and Stoic mental models.
- **Part 3** delivers the rigid, practical 'Unhackable Protocols' engineered for immediate lifestyle integration tomorrow morning.

This is the New Immortality—an elite neuro-philosophical framework that safely anchors your biology inside an eternal, unmoving sanctuary of joy and establishes an impregnable Inner Citadel within your destiny. The path to reclaim the throne of your sovereign consciousness initiates right here, right now. Let the journey begin.

PART 1

The Wired Brain & The Modern Crisis

LESSON 1

The Chaos of the Cursor

Introduction: The Restlessness of the Cursor and the Human Mind

Today, our mornings do not begin with the natural light of the sun or the gentle sound of birds. Instead, they start with the sharp, intrusive 'ping' of a smartphone that directly strikes our sleeping brain. The very first action we perform upon opening our eyes is reaching out to touch a glass screen. When we watch that tiny arrow—the cursor—move across a computer monitor, or when we endlessly scroll down a social media feed with our thumbs, it superficially appears as though we are connecting with the world, our friends, and our work. However, just beneath the surface of this simple action, a profound and invisible chaos is taking birth within human consciousness and the architecture of the brain.

This cursor is not merely moving across a digital screen; it is actively fracturing the subtle layers of our attention span. The greatest crisis of the current generation is not a lack of opportunities, but rather the hard truth that our own attention is no longer under our control. From the glass-paneled cabins of corporate offices to the quiet bedrooms of college students, this digital cursor is silently dictating human decisions. When we unlock our phones every two minutes without any valid reason, we have essentially surrendered our willpower to that digital entity.

The Dopamine Loop: The Chemical That Hacks Our Brain

To reach the root of this restlessness, we must step into the laboratories of modern neuroscience. Inside the human brain exists a highly potent neurotransmitter called **Dopamine**. In everyday conversation, people often mistakenly label it as the 'pleasure hormone.' From a scientific standpoint, this is fundamentally incorrect. Dopamine does not reward you with happiness *after* a task is completed. Instead, it creates the intense **anticipation, expectation, and craving** to perform that task. It is the chemical of reward-seeking.

During primitive times, when humans lived in wild jungles, this dopamine pathway was essential for survival. It motivated early humans to hunt for food and search for water sources. When they successfully found berries or prey, dopamine spiked, reinforcing the brain's memory so they would know exactly where to return the next time hunger struck. Unfortunately, modern tech conglomerates have meticulously engineered their applications to hack this exact, ancient biological mechanism.

Today, this psychological trap operates in four distinct stages, universally known as **'The Dopamine Loop'**:

1. **The Trigger:** Your phone screen suddenly flashes, or a notification bell rings. This serves as an immediate neurological cue to your brain that something 'new' or 'exciting' awaits you.
2. **The Action:** The moment this trigger occurs, a craving is generated within. You abandon your important task, reach out your hand, and pick up the device.
3. **The Variable Reward:** When you look at the screen, it could be an urgent business email, a new like from a friend, or

simply a useless advertisement. Neuroscience proves that if the reward is 'variable'—meaning unpredictable and different every single time—dopamine spikes to its absolute highest levels. This is precisely how a slot machine operates in a casino. A gambler pulls the lever repeatedly because they do not know if the next turn will hit the jackpot. You scroll for the exact same psychological reason.

4. **The Endless Investment:** Once you receive that tiny burst of chemical reward, your brain hardwires that behavioral pathway. You continue to scroll deeper down the feed to hunt for the next unpredictable reward. The cycle closes, and the loop never truly ends.

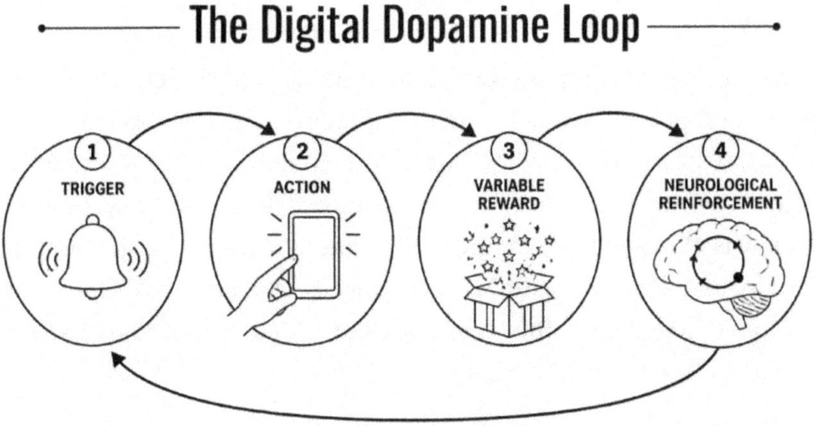

The Endless Dopamine Loop — How variable rewards artificially hijack human neural pathways to create screen addiction.

'Attention Overload' and the Cognitive Toll of the Cursor

When this dopamine loop is repeated hundreds of times throughout a single day, the human brain enters a state of severe **'Attention Overload.'** The human mind was never evolutionarily designed to process a brand-new piece of information, a new face, or a new psychological stressor every five seconds. When you are viewing a corporate email, reading global news in an adjacent tab, and simultaneously replying to social media messages on your phone, your brain expends an immense amount of energy trying to keep up with the physical movement of your cursor.

This constant mental fragmentation takes a direct toll on our capacity for Deep Work. Slowly but surely, our cognitive focus becomes so severely degraded that we find ourselves unable to read a single page of a physical book without reflexively reaching for our phones. This is the precise chaos of the cursor that leaves us feeling perpetually exhausted, irritable, and hollow from within.

Ancient Perspectives: The Untamed 'Monkey Mind'

When we discuss modern attention deficits or chronic mental distraction, it is easy to assume that this crisis belongs exclusively to the 21st century. However, if we turn the pages of history and look at ancient world philosophies, we discover that this psychological ailment is thousands of years old. In ancient Indian philosophy and the Upanishads, a beautiful and highly accurate metaphor was developed to explain this restless state of consciousness: **'Markat Nyaya'**, or the **'Monkey Mind.'**

The ancient seers compared the human mind to a monkey that is naturally restless by its very definition. It can never sit quietly in one place. Now, imagine that specific monkey is intoxicated with wine, stung by a venomous scorpion, and possessed by an unseen spirit. That monkey would writhe in agony, jumping frantically from one branch to another without any true purpose or direction. According to timeless wisdom, the untrained human mind behaves in this exact manner.

In our current digital era, this ancient metaphor applies to us with absolute, one-hundred-percent precision:

- **The Natural Monkey:** Our baseline human mind.
- **The Intoxicating Wine:** The endless stream of digital dopamine from the internet.
- **The Scorpion's Sting:** Corporate stress, hyper-competition, and the pain of constant comparison.
- **The Unseen Spirit:** FOMO (Fear of Missing Out) — the haunting anxiety that we are being left behind.

In ancient times, practices like deep meditation, breathwork, and structured concentration were taught to tame this inner monkey. The modern tragedy, however, is that the tech corporations designing our apps have deeply studied this 'monkey mind.' They actively profit by keeping our attention fragmented. When your cursor switches tabs or jumps from Instagram to YouTube, your internal monkey is simply leaping across digital branches. What modern neuroscience terms 'Cognitive Switching Cost'—the destruction of brain energy caused by constantly shifting focus—our ancestors long ago labeled as the 'restlessness of the consciousness' (Chitta Vyagrata). The problem remains identical; only the tool has evolved from primal distractions into a smartphone.

Corporate Burnout and the Trap of Silent Stress

Let us now examine this digital chaos through the lens of the corporate world, where the cursor has practically become a symbol of unseen servitude. Modern corporate culture frequently utilizes a highly dangerous term: **'Burnout.'** Burnout is not merely physical fatigue. It is a profound psychological and emotional state where an individual feels that no matter how hard they exert themselves, it is never enough. They begin to feel entirely depleted and hollowed out from the inside.

In neurological terms, when an employee sits in front of a computer screen for a continuous 9-to-5 grind, their cursor is not the only thing moving. Their brain is being kept in a perpetual state of **'Fight or Flight'** mode. Our email inboxes have effectively become the modern equivalent of the primal jungle. In ancient times, when a human faced a wild predator, the brain immediately released stress hormones like **Cortisol** and **Adrenaline** to ensure immediate survival. Once the predator left, the stress response naturally deactivated.

However, in a modern corporate setting:

- A harsh email from a manager or an unexpected message from a client acts as that exact wild predator.
- The critical issue is that this digital predator never leaves the jungle. Even after the laptop is closed, push notifications keep arriving on our personal devices.
- Consequently, cortisol levels within the brain never get the opportunity to reset. In medicine, this is defined as **'Chronic Stress'** or silent stress.

When this silent stress persists for weeks and months, a vital region of the brain called the **Prefrontal Cortex** begins to physically atrophy and weaken. This is the exact area responsible for executive decision-making, emotional regulation, and creative thinking. When the prefrontal cortex experiences severe exhaustion, an individual can still physically perform tasks, but their deeper cognitive efficiency vanishes. They become chronically anxious, suffer from insomnia despite being physically exhausted, and begin to drag themselves through life entirely dependent on artificial stimulants like caffeine.

Primitive Stress vs. Modern Corporate Stress — Why the human brain is evolutionarily unequipped for 24/7 digital input.

Generation Z and the New Frontier of Mental Health

In the final phase of this chapter, we must direct our focus toward the generation that was born directly into this digitized ecosystem—**Generation Z (Gen-Z)**. This demographic has never known a world devoid of smartphones or high-speed connectivity. Superficial observers often view this youth culture as immensely privileged, citing their instant access to the entire sum of human knowledge at a single click. Yet, deep academic research and global metrics paint a starkly terrifying reality.

Today's youth represent the most interconnected generation in human history, yet the ultimate irony remains that they are statistically the most isolated, lonely, and anxious generation to ever exist. The primary catalyst for this crisis is **the illusion of reality presented through digital screens**.

The moment a young individual opens a social media application, they are immediately confronted with the curated 'Highlight Reels' of other people's lives. Someone is showcasing an expensive vehicle, while another is documenting a luxurious vacation. According to neuroscience, the human brain possesses an involuntary evolutionary mechanism known as **'Social Comparison.'** Our brains are biologically wired to measure our own self-worth against our peer group. When an eighteen or twenty-year-old is continuously subjected to this synthetic brilliance, their subconscious mind internalizes a toxic message: "I am falling behind." This has been officially termed **'FOMO' (Fear of Missing Out).**

This perpetual comparison acts like a silent parasite, slowly eating away at their self-esteem from within. Digital 'likes' and 'comments' become their primary source of neurological dopamine. When a posted photo fails to accumulate the anticipated number of interactions, dopamine levels within the brain crash abruptly. This sudden drop triggers deep waves of inadequacy, severe digital anxiety, and clinical depression. They are running blindly behind a digital cursor that never grants them a moment of peace.

CONCLUSION: From the Cursor to Consciousness

The deep research presented across this opening chapter illuminates one undeniable fact: Technology itself is not the enemy; our unmonitored, blind dependency on it is. The cursor racing across our screens is simply exploiting the evolutionary vulnerabilities of our biological brain to turn us into digital consumers. While modern science explicitly maps out how our dopamine loops function and why we fall victim to burnout, our ancient wisdom reminds us that this mental restlessness is an age-old battle—one that we are fully equipped to win.

The purpose of this book is not to force you to throw away your technology or isolate yourself in remote mountains. The core takeaway of this first chapter is that until you consciously comprehend exactly how your brain is being hacked, you will never possess the power to 'unhack' it.

A Personal Message from Hanika Deepchand

My dear readers, the moment you truly observe and understand the chaos of this screen, you cease to be a slave to the cursor; you become the sovereign master of your own attention. Authentic fulfillment and emotional resilience do not exist within an external device or a software notification. They reside deep within that quiet, untouchable center of your being—a sacred space that no digital screen can ever hack. It is time to step out of the chaos of the cursor and reclaim the absolute power of your consciousness.

LESSON 2

Tired but Wired

Introduction: The Mystery of the 'Tired but Wired' Phenomenon

The supreme irony of modern existence is that the average contemporary human expends almost zero physical energy throughout the day. We sit in climate-controlled environments, rest on ergonomically padded chairs, and commute in motorized vehicles. Yet, the moment we lay down on our beds at night, our physical bodies feel completely broken, our eyes feel intensely heavy, but our minds refuse to shut down. We experience a state of profound exhaustion, yet the exact second we close our eyes, an unstoppable storm of racing thoughts ignites within our consciousness. In modern neuroscience, this debilitating state is precisely classified as the **'Tired but Wired'** phenomenon.

This is a neurological state where your physical biology is begging for recuperation, but your Central Nervous System is stuck operating in an Emergency Mode. To escape this invisible cage, individuals reflexively resort to sleeping pills, late-night screen scrolling, or alcohol. What they fail to comprehend is that the root cause of this suffering is not an external illness, but rather the severe dysregulation of two primary biological mechanisms within their own skulls: **the disruption of Cortisol cycles** and the activation of an **'Amygdala Hijack.'**

Silent Stress and the Cortisol Tsunami

Our biology utilizes highly sophisticated internal clocks and chemical pathways to regulate daily performance. Chief among these chemicals is **Cortisol**, globally recognized as the primary stress hormone. Evolution beautifully designed a natural rhythm for cortisol production, directly synchronized with the planet's day-and-night cycle, known as the **Circadian Rhythm**.

- **The Evolutionary Design:** Under optimal conditions, cortisol production spikes dramatically in the early morning hours to provide the human organism with the vital alertness and energy required to start the day. As daylight recedes and night approaches, cortisol levels are engineered to gradually cascade downward, allowing **Melatonin** (the sleep hormone) to flood the brain and initiate deep rest.
- **The Modern Crisis (Silent Stress):** Due to the hyper-connected architecture of modern corporate landscapes, perpetual email notifications, looming project deadlines, and the implicit obligation to remain constantly reachable, the human brain never genuinely feels 'safe.' When a manager dispatches a text message at 9:00 PM, your primitive biology perceives that notification as an immediate threat to survival. Consequently, under this sustained 'silent stress,' the necessary nighttime drop in cortisol never occurs.

When cortisol remains artificially elevated during your sleeping hours, melatonin is biologically blocked from performing its job. The direct neurological consequence is that you spend hours tossing and turning in your bed. Your body is fundamentally exhausted (Tired) because your daily mental battery has been completely drained, but your neurological framework remains entirely hyper-active and bound (Wired).

Amygdala Hijack: When the Brain's Alarm Refuses to Turn Off

Deep within the temporal lobes of the human brain lies an almond-shaped cluster of nuclei known as the **Amygdala**. This structure serves as our evolutionary security guard—the biological fire alarm of the brain. Its currents and primitive mandate are to scan the immediate environment for existential threats and trigger survival behaviors.

Thousands of years ago, when an early human encountered a predatory animal in the wild, the amygdala activated instantaneously. It immediately commandeered the entire brain, effectively bypassing the rational, decision-making region—the **Prefrontal Cortex**—so the individual could fight or flee without losing precious seconds to conscious thought. Celebrated psychologist Daniel Goleman officially classified this primitive neurological takeover as an **'Amygdala Hijack.'**

In our modern corporate ecosystem, there are no saber-toothed tigers, yet your amygdala processes the following digital inputs as identical existential threats:

1. **The Inundated Email Inbox:** Every unread notification is interpreted by the amygdala as an incoming attack.
2. **The Pressure of Unrealistic Targets:** The underlying fear of unemployment or professional failure forces the amygdala to sound its survival siren indefinitely.
3. **Digital Anxiety and Comparison:** A critical comment or a lack of digital validation on social platforms triggers an ancient biological fear of social banishment.

The critical flaw in our modern world is that while the primitive predator eventually left the area, allowing the amygdala to reset, our digital predators never leave the jungle. When you attempt to sleep at night, your brain is still trapped in a state of active Amygdala Hijack. It is continuously broadcasting an internal emergency signal to your body: "Do not sleep, the danger is still present." This is the precise reason you remain wide awake despite profound physical fatigue.

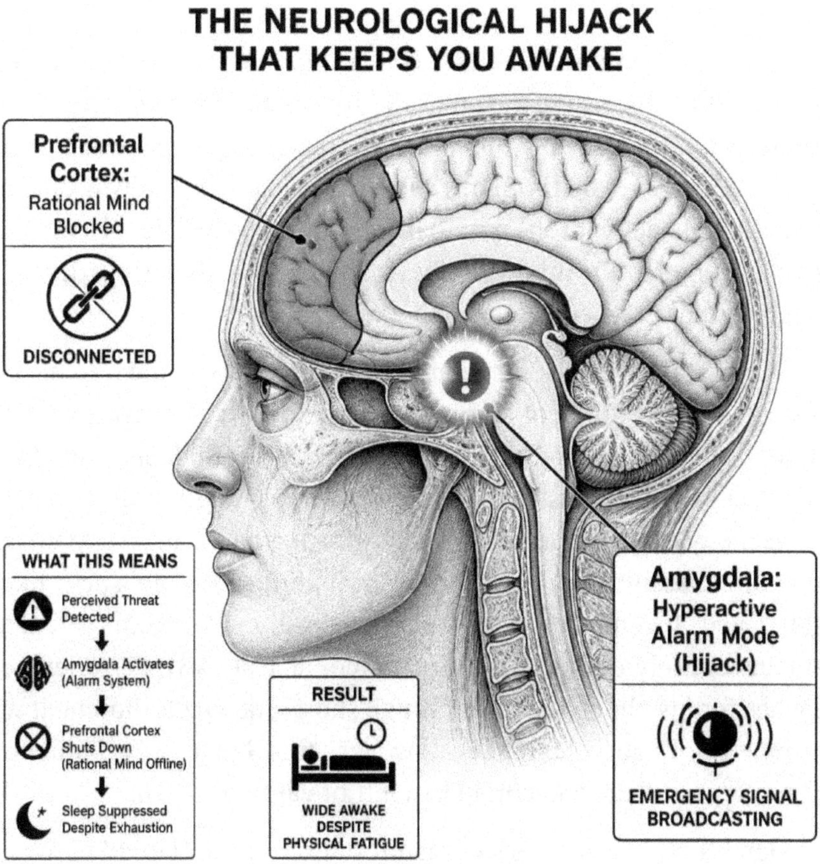

The Neurology of an Amygdala Hijack — How the brain's internal alarm system systematically blocks executive function and rest.

Real-Life Case Study: *Harsh and the Corporate Rat Race Trap*

To comprehend this phenomenon with greater depth, let us examine the case of 32-year-old Harsh (Assumed Name), a Senior Project Manager at a major technology firm in Delhi. On the surface, Harsh's life looks incredibly successful—a high salary, a beautiful apartment, and social prestige. Yet behind this external glamour, Harsh has been fighting a silent and terrifying psychological battle for the past two years.

Every morning at 9:00 AM, Harsh logs into his laptop. His day ignites with consecutive meetings, high-pressure client demands, and the manual motion of moving a digital cursor across infinite spreadsheets. By 7:00 PM, he is entirely depleted, both physically and mentally. His neck throbs with pain and his eyes feel deeply fatigued from the aggressive glow of the monitor. But the story does not conclude there.

When Harsh returns home at 10:00 PM and lays down in his bed to sleep, the true torment begins. He switches off the lights, rests his head on the pillow, and attempts to drift away. Suddenly, his brain enters an unprovoked state of hyper-activity. The pending reports for the next day, a critical remark made by his manager, and a teammate's incomplete assignment start racing through his consciousness like a high-speed locomotive. He feels physically shattered, yet sleep remains entirely out of reach. Frustrated, at 1:00 AM, he reflexively reaches for his phone to scroll through short video reels, hoping it will distract his racing thoughts. However, this habit only obliterates whatever tiny chance his brain had left of calming down.

Harsh's reality is a perfect manifestation of the 'Tired but Wired' loop. His physical biology is crying out for deep rest, but his neurological pathways are still hyper-actively running laps at his corporate office desk.

The Demise of the Circadian Rhythm and Melatonin Suppression

Let us dive into the deeper scientific layers of exactly what occurs inside the human organism when individuals like Sumit are trapped in this midnight cycle. Through millions of years of evolutionary development, our bodies built an internal biological clock known in medical science as the **Circadian Rhythm**. This clock operates in flawless synchronization with the natural transitions of solar light and planetary darkness.

As the sun sets and twilight deepens, specialized cells in our eyes transmit a vital signal to the **Pineal Gland** nested deep inside the brain. Upon receiving this message, the gland immediately synthesizes and releases **Melatonin**, universally recognized as the sleep hormone. Melatonin's primary mandate is to lower core body temperature, decrease heart rate, and signals the entire central nervous system that it is officially safe to surrender to recovery.

However, the contemporary digital and corporate ecosystem has systematically demolished this natural clock due to two massive catalysts:

1. The Deception of Artificial Blue Light

When we work late on laptops or hold mobile screens inches away from our faces in bed, these devices emit a highly concentrated frequency of **Blue Light**. This artificial spectrum strikes the retina directly. The biological regulator of our circadian rhythm—the Suprachiasmatic Nucleus (SCN)—gets completely deceived by this frequency. It interprets the blue light as broad daylight, concluding that it is mid-afternoon. Consequently, the pineal gland abruptly halts the production of melatonin. Your body simply remains unaware that night has fallen.

2. The Artificial Spike of Cortisol

As explored earlier, while a morning cortisol spike is essential, a nighttime drop is non-negotiable for sleep. When you check corporate emails at midnight or stress over professional obligations, your hyperactive amygdala commands your adrenal glands to trigger an unseasonal spike of cortisol. It is an unyielding law of human biology: **the absolute moment cortisol levels are elevated, melatonin levels plummet to zero.** These two chemicals are biologically incapable of working simultaneously. This is precisely why you spend your nights counting the seconds, as your internal neurological chemistry fights an active, invisible war against itself.

Screen Addiction and Neurological Fatigue

When the human brain remains trapped in this 'Tired but Wired' state for an extended duration, a secondary pathology manifests, known in neuroscience as **Neurological Fatigue**. This is fundamentally distinct from ordinary physical exhaustion. When you exercise or run, your muscular fibers fatigue, and simple physical rest completely restores them. However, when you operate before a glowing screen for 10 to 12 hours a day, your muscular skeletal system isn't the primary victim—your neural pathways are.

Our brains contain billions of neurons that constantly transmit information via delicate electrical impulses. When we subject our minds to an unrelenting onslaught of information overload—such as managing multiple browser tabs, rapidly switching reels, and monitoring corporate chat feeds—these neurons are forced to fire at an unsustainably high frequency. This metabolic hyper-activity results in the accumulation of a toxic byproduct within the brain tissue called **Adenosine**.

Under normal evolutionary parameters, the buildup of adenosine acts as an internal pressure gauge that induces deep sleep, allowing the brain's unique cleaning system (the glymphatic system) to wash away this metabolic waste overnight. But when we remain chained to digital screens past midnight, the brain is robbed of this essential cleaning window. The next morning, you wake up with a brain that is already drowning in yesterday's cognitive waste. This chronic state of neurological fatigue forces the tired brain to crave even heavier doses of artificial dopamine, trapping the individual in a vicious cycle of screen addiction.

The Physical Vectors of Burnout: When the Body Rejects the Strain

It is absolutely imperative to recognize that this state of perpetual mental tension does not confine itself within the limits of the skull. The mind and body operate as an interconnected loop. When the amygdala is subjected to a permanent hijack and cortisol levels refuse to subside at night, the physical architecture of the human organism eventually breaks down under the weight of corporate burnout.

If you have been navigating this cycle for an extended period, your physical biology will inevitably begin to trigger four distinct warning signals:

1. **Chronic Neuromuscular Pain:** When the brain perceives a state of permanent threat, it involuntarily triggers a state of sustained muscle contraction. Chronic tightness in the shoulders, persistent neck stiffness, and the unconscious clenching of the jaw during sleep are direct physical responses to this psychological state.
2. **The Gut-Brain Axis Disruption:** Modern medicine confirms that the human gastrointestinal tract serves as our 'second brain.' When systemic cortisol remains elevated, the brain actively diverts blood flow away from the digestive organs. This chronic restriction triggers severe acid reflux, chronic indigestion, and a permanent sensation of abdominal heaviness.
3. **Resting Heart Rate Fluctuations:** Experiencing sudden palpitations or an elevated resting heart rate while sitting

completely still is definitive diagnostic proof that your Sympathetic Nervous System is running entirely unmonitored.

4. **Suppressed Immunological Defense:** While acute cortisol temporary manages inflammation, chronic systemic exposure severely degrades your white blood cells. Consequently, individuals suffering from burnout experience a drastic drop in immunity, making them highly susceptible to frequent viral infections, prolonged colds, and extended recovery windows.

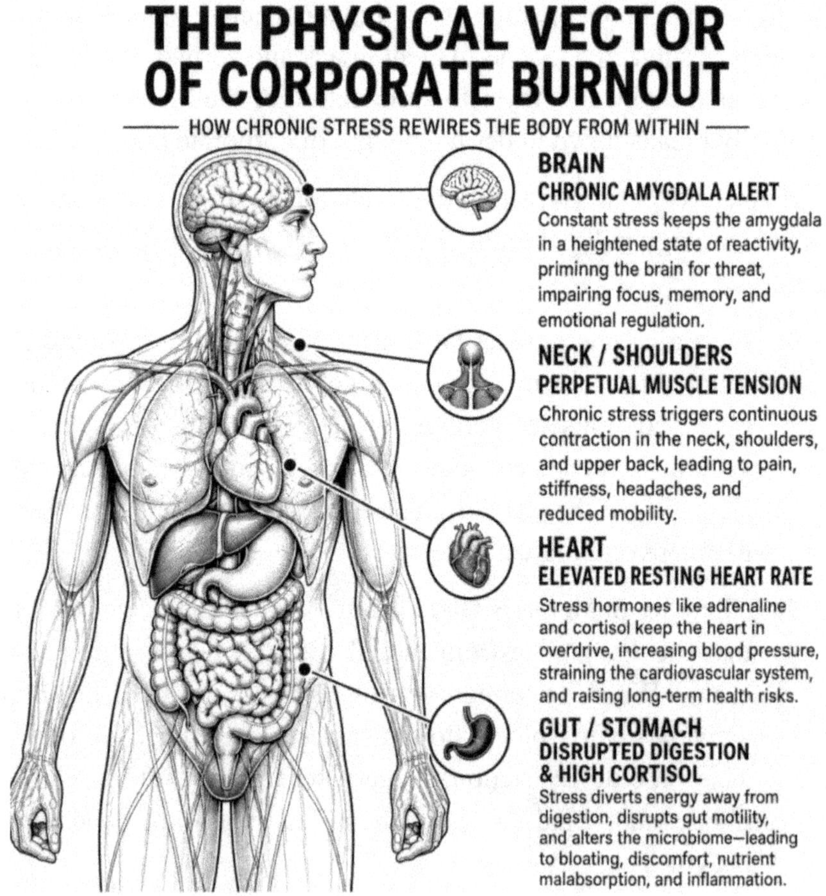

The Physical Map of Burnout — How chronic digital stress translates into systemic physiological illness.

CONCLUSION: The Science of Quieting the Alarm

The deep neurological evaluation presented across this second chapter clearly demonstrates that being 'Tired but Wired' is not a personal failure or simple fatigue; it is a severe systemic imbalance of your brain's evolutionary defense network. Until we consciously deactivate this hyperactive amygdala alarm, shut down the deception of artificial blue light, and restore the natural baseline of our cortisol rhythm, no premium mattress or external sleeping aid can provide genuine restoration. Escaping the loop of burnout fundamentally begins with the conscious realization that our biological systems require structured periods of absolute unavailability.

A Personal Message from Hanika Deepchand

My dear readers, your brain is a highly complex biological organ, not an industrialized machine designed to run twenty-four hours a day. If your mind continues to race long after you have gone to bed, cease being angry with yourself. Understand that your internal security guard—your amygdala—is simply trying its best to protect you from perceived corporate and digital threats. It is merely executing its evolutionary duty. But now, the moment has arrived for you to consciously reclaim your sovereignty. The absolute second you establish non-negotiable digital boundaries at night and deeply reassure your subconscious mind that your daily work is officially completed, you are entirely safe, and you are permitted to rest—that exhausted, anxious mind will finally surrender to the profound, healing embrace of deep sleep.

LESSON 3

The Comparison Trap

Introduction: The Invisible War Behind the Screen

In this third decade of the 21st century, the largest psychological experiment in human history is actively underway. This experiment is not being conducted in a traditional laboratory; rather, it takes place on the five-inch glowing screens held firmly in our hands. The current youth, specifically Generation Z (Gen-Z), breathe in a reality where their digital presence frequently carries far more weight than their physical existence. Before looking in a physical mirror each morning, a young individual reflexively checks their virtual ecosystem to see how their digital worth has shifted overnight.

However, this unrelenting connectivity demands a severe psychological toll. On the surface, social media platforms advertise themselves as tools designed to connect the entire world. In reality, they are triggering a profound inner vacuum and persistent mental unrest. As we view the perfectly curated lives, exotic vacations, luxury vehicles, and flawless smiles of others through a glass filter, an invisible, silent, and continuous war ignites within our subconscious. This psychological phenomenon is universally defined as 'The

Comparison Trap.' It functions as a complex labyrinth. Once an individual falls into its currents, their innate, natural happiness is systematically hacked.

The Neuroscience of Social Media Anxiety

To truly comprehend the depth of this comparison trap, we must analyze the evolutionary history of the human brain, which developed over millions of years. Our brain is, by its biological design, a 'comparative machine.' In primitive eras, when humans operated within small tribal communities, it was evolutionarily vital to monitor one's standing relative to the rest of the group. Social acceptance meant physical survival and security, whereas social rejection or banishment from the tribe meant certain death. Therefore, the human mind continuously evaluates itself by observing others.

According to modern neuroscience, the moment we open a social media application, our brain instantly activates this primitive tribal survival mechanism. The modern crisis, however, lies in scale. In ancestral times, our tribe consisted of merely 50 to 100 individuals against whom we measured our worth. Today, through global networks, our tribe has artificially expanded to include the entire planet. A twenty-year-old student sitting alone in their bedroom is now actively measuring their life against global celebrities or hyper-wealthy peers halfway across the world.

When the brain chronically perceives itself as inferior during these comparisons, a specific region responsible for registering physical pain and social threat—the **Anterior Cingulate Cortex**—becomes hyper-active. The brain processes this digital inferiority as a literal 'physical injury' or a profound existential threat. Consequently, severe social anxiety and deep-seated feelings of inadequacy are generated. You are physically safe in your room, yet your neurological framework is continuously broadcasting an alarm: "You are falling behind; your standing in the tribe is dangerously compromised."

The Mathematics of Likes and the Economy of Synthetic Self-Esteem

Social media architectures are meticulously engineered to lock human self-esteem onto quantifiable metrics. The count of likes, comments, and shares on a post are not merely neutral numbers; they function as a form of **'Digital Currency'** for our neurological pathways.

The moment a young individual shares a photograph or a video on a public feed, a tense period of anticipation grips their brain. They compulsively check their device every two minutes to monitor the numerical growth of their interactions.

- **When Likes Accumulate:** The brain's neurological reward center (the Ventral Striatum) experiences an artificial surge of dopamine. The individual experiences a transient sensation of social validation, feeling important and accepted by the tribe.
- **When Likes Fail to Manifest:** Dopamine levels abruptly crash far below the baseline. In neurobiology, this chemical drop is classified as a **'Dopamine Crash.'**

Due to the artificial volatility of this chemical cycle, a young person's core self-esteem becomes entirely externalized, surrendered to the whims of a digital audience. If complete strangers click a button, they feel validated; if the metric stalls, they internalize a toxic narrative that they are physically unappealing, unsuccessful, and worthless. This creates a dangerous economy of synthetic self-esteem where individuals trade their authentic identity to become absolute slaves to a digital thumbs-up.

The Science of FOMO: The Terror of Missing Out

The most lethal weapon deployed by this comparison trap is **FOMO (Fear of Missing Out)**. This is far more than a contemporary slang term; it represents a documented, severe psychological distress pattern.

Consider a Saturday evening where you are resting peacefully in your home or focused on your studies. The exact moment you open your device and witness photographs of peers laughing, dancing, and documenting a social gathering, a profound wave of anxiety overrides your peace. Your brain instantly succumbs to a cognitive illusion: the narrative that the entire world is enjoying an exquisite existence, and you are the solitary failure wasting your life within a confined space.

This fear of missing out triggers an evolutionary stress response akin to an **existential threat**. The rational mind fails to process that no one documents their moments of profound grief, domestic arguments, or personal failures on a public feed. We reflexively compare our messy, unedited, 'behind-the-scenes' reality with the polished, hyper-filtered 'highlight reels' of others. This is an entirely asymmetrical and rigged competition—one where your psychological defeat is mathematically guaranteed. This ongoing illusion actively extracts the natural, baseline happiness that can only be accessed by remaining content within the present moment.

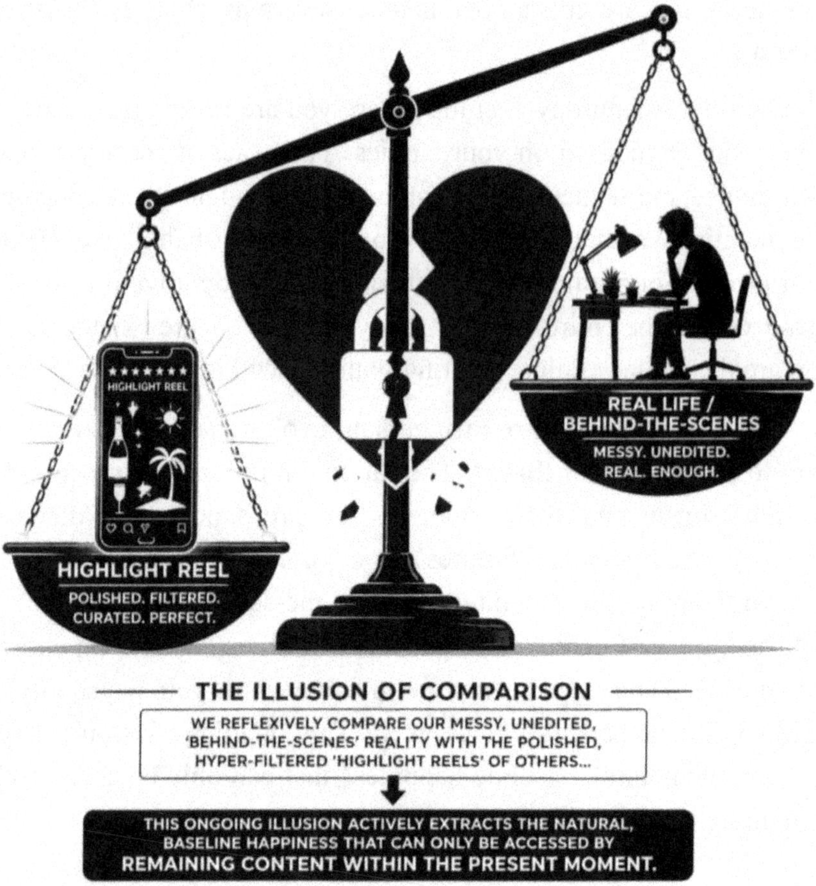

The Scale of Social Comparison — How our cognitive architecture miscalculates personal worth by weighing physical reality against digital illusions.

Hyper-Reality and the Labyrinth of Digital Beauty Standards

In our contemporary era, the comparison trap has extended past lifestyles and geographic destinations; it has directly penetrated the perception of our physical anatomy. Modern sociology utilizes the term **'Hyper-Reality'** to define this crisis. It represents a synthetic, simulated world that appears significantly more beautiful, flawless, and 'perfect' than physical reality itself, causing the human subconscious to accept the simulation as the ultimate truth.

Digital camera filters and advanced AI-driven beautification tools have birthed this hyper-real ecosystem. When an individual captures an image within an application, the underlying algorithm instantly and invisibly alters reality:

- It completely obliterates facial blemishes and structural asymmetry.
- It unnaturally enlarges the optical framework, adding artificial luminescence.
- It completely recalibrates skin tones and bodily proportions.

The psychological pathology ignites when a person continuously measures their physical, unedited face in a morning mirror against the hyper-real, filtered avatar on their screen. Clinical psychiatric research has identified a rising manifestation known as **'Snapchat Dysmorphia.'** This represents a severe body dysmorphic state where youths develop an intense aversion to their organic anatomy. They become so deeply trapped within this hyper-real labyrinth that they lose the basic psychological courage to present an unaltered image of themselves to the world. It systematically hacks the innate self-acceptance and natural beauty given to us by biology.

The Algorithmic Architecture: Monetizing the Labyrinth

We must expose a critical, clinical truth within our deep research: the comparison trap is not a cultural accident. It has been intentionally, systematically engineered by some of the most sophisticated software minds on earth. The proprietary **algorithms** fueling social platforms operate with a singular, unyielding objective—**'User Attention Optimization.'** Their goal is to maximize the minutes your eyes remain glued to the glass pane.

Internal corporate research within tech conglomerates has long proven that the human brain does not sustain engagement on content that induces peace, safety, or simple contentment. Instead, human neurology lingers significantly longer on stimuli that provoke **insecurity, outrage, or comparison**.

- When you view a piece of media that covertly signals a personal deficiency, your attention locks onto it.
- You linger on the screen, searching for methods or products to rectify that perceived inadequacy.
- The algorithm registers this specific psychological vulnerability instantly, continuously flooding your feed with identical imagery and hyper-targeted advertisements (such as weight-loss placebos, cosmetic interventions, or luxury consumer products).

To state it bluntly: **your psychological unrest and digital insecurity represent billions of dollars in net corporate profit.** These platforms require you to remain perpetually locked in comparison, feeling internally fragmented, because an insecure, anxious human being is the most hyper-consumptive demographic in existence. The moment you comprehend the explicit economic model behind the screen, you take your first sovereign step out of the labyrinth.

Real-Life Case Study: *The Digital Cage of 21-Year-Old Riya*

To map this psychological pathology into real-world terms, let us examine the reality of Riya (Assumed Name), a 21-year-old college student living in Mumbai. Academically, Riya is highly accomplished, possesses an inherently warm demeanor, and belongs to a profoundly supportive family unit. Yet, over the past twelve months, Riya has been navigating a severe, quiet wave of clinical anxiety and isolation.

Every night before sleeping, Riya compulsively engages with Instagram. Across her feed, she observes peers of her exact demographic showcasing luxury designer apparel, dining at elite venues, and flaunting physically 'perfect' bodies. Unconsciously, Riya's mind initiates an immediate social comparison. She begins to view her natural skin tone as inadequate, her personal wardrobe as embarrassingly ordinary, and her entire life path as profoundly stagnant.

To cope with this surging feeling of inferiority, Riya began altering her own digital presence, deploying heavy algorithmic filters across every image she shared. Eventually, her entire psychological worth became hyper-focused on a singular index: the specific volume of comments under her posts. On a recent evening, after sharing a highly orchestrated photograph, the metric failed to hit her anticipated target. The sudden dopamine crash triggered a severe, acute panic attack. She internalized a distorted narrative that she was socially repulsive and universally rejected by her peers. Riya's reality is the lived reality of millions of Gen-Z youths. They are locked within a digital cage, having willingly surrendered the keys to a corporate algorithm.

CONCLUSION: Escaping the Labyrinth

The deep evaluation presented across this third chapter confirms that the comparison trap is not a benign habit; it is a highly sophisticated, modern technological exploitation of our brain's ancient social machinery. Until we actively demystify the hyper-reality presented on our feeds, decode the economic models of algorithms, and completely untether our human self-worth from numerical digital metrics, reclaiming authentic, natural happiness remains a biological impossibility. The definitive step out of this labyrinth begins with the conscious realization that everything that glitters on a digital screen is a monetized illusion.

A Personal Message from Hanika Deepchand

My dear readers, your intrinsic human value is not determined by whether a corporate algorithm or an absolute stranger across a digital network chooses to 'like' your face or your life path. The universe has engineered you as an absolute, completely non-replicable masterpiece. The moment you look at someone else's curated, hyper-filtered digital illusion and conclude that your real, organic life is inferior, you are actively insulting your own consciousness. Break this comparison trap today. Place your device face down, close your physical eyes, and tune into the absolute depth of your breath. This real life, this unedited present moment, is infinitely more precious than any digital metric or social media race. Refuse to let your natural happiness be hacked for someone else's corporate profit, because within your authentic, unfiltered self, you are already entirely complete, completely unique, and profoundly enough.

LESSON 4

Connected yet Alone

Introduction: The Crowd of the Virtual World and the Real Vacuum

In this current phase of the 21st century, human civilization has achieved a milestone that would have been deemed utterly impossible just fifty years ago. We are living in the most hyper-connected era in human history. At the casual stroke of a finger on a glass pane, we can instantaneously speak to an individual stationed on the exact opposite side of the planet. Platforms like Facebook, Instagram, and WhatsApp enable users to hoard 5,000 or more 'followers' and digital 'friends.' To a superficial observer, it would appear that the modern human is structurally incapable of experiencing isolation, given the 24-hour virtual army standing at their disposal.

Yet, the moment we look past the aggressive luminescence of the digital display and peer into the internal chambers of human hearts, a terrifying and bitter reality exposes itself. Today's generation represents the most hyper-connected demographic to ever walk the earth, yet they simultaneously represent the most isolated, lonely, and emotionally detached generation in human history. At two o'clock in the morning, while the screen flashes with dozens of real-time notifications, individuals lie frozen in their beds experiencing a crushing sense of emptiness. They look at the device and ask a silent, haunting question: why is it that in this sea of 5,000 digital entities, there is not a single soul with whom I can share my authentic suffering without wearing a synthetic mask? This is the agonizing pathology we define as being 'Connected yet Alone.'

Hyper-Connectivity and the Neurology of Loneliness

To dissect this profound internal vacuum, we must evaluate the empirical findings of modern neuroscience laboratories. The human brain, through millions of years of evolutionary engineering, was built exclusively for physical, face-to-face human interaction. When two individuals sit across from one another, engage in unedited eye contact, process the vocal frequencies of speech, and share physical proximity, the brain synthesizes and floods the system with a hormone called **Oxytocin**. Known as the 'bonding neurotransmitter,' oxytocin is biologically responsible for creating sensations of safety, deep tranquility, and authentic psychological trust.

However, when we converse with an individual via a text interface or trade likes and comments across a social media feed, we are engaging in a **'Synthetic Connection'** (artificial bond). Digital communication strips away optical synchronization; it entirely robs our neurology of the ability to read non-verbal body language, micro-expressions, and biophysical energy. Neuroscience proves that our ancient biological systems refuse to recognize these artificial pixels as a genuine human relationship.

Instead of nurturing our neurobiology with oxytocin (profound relationship), social media feeds us cheap, short-lived spikes of dopamine (momentary stimulation). The chronic result is that an individual can interact with hundreds of digital avatars throughout the day—leaving their brain severely overloaded with raw information—

while their deeper emotional core remains completely starved of biological nourishment. This is the mechanism of **Biological Loneliness**. You possess 5,000 online connections, yet your brain is neurologically registering isolated abandonment because it is being deprived of the organic human contact it was evolutionarily designed to receive.

The Metric Illusion: The Devaluation of Human Bonds into Numbers

We must explicitly dissect how digital architectures have systematically commodified sacred human relationships into sterile numerical values. In our current era, the depth of an individual's social bond is no longer evaluated by whether they will stand by your side during an acute life crisis. Instead, it is measured by whether they clicked 'like' on your latest update, viewed your transient 24-hour story, or left an automated comment on your feed.

The exact moment human relationships are converted into numbers, authentic and vulnerable dialogue is instantly destroyed. We begin to aggressively sanitize our real flaws, edit out our domestic sorrows, and conceal our everyday struggles because corporate algorithms only promote images of artificial perfection. We build a highly manufactured **Digital Persona** that appears permanently blissful, hyper-successful, and physically striking.

The profound tragedy lies here: society begins to fall in love with your polished digital ghost, causing your authentic, unedited self to sink deeper into absolute isolation. You become paralyzed by an underlying fear that if the virtual crowd ever witnesses your raw reality—your corporate stress, your financial insecurities, and your ordinary, unfiltered life—they will instantly vanish and leave you behind. This devaluation of relationships into digital metrics is the silent foundation of modern clinical depression.

The Digital Cage — How thousands of hyper-virtual connections leave the authentic human observer entirely isolated and emotionally starved.

Real-Life Case Study: *The Virtual Mirage of 25-Year-Old Kabir*

To study this psychological pathology in real-world dimensions, let us examine the lived reality of 25-year-old Kabir (Assumed Name), a software engineer operating within an elite information technology firm in Bengaluru. Across the digital universe, Kabir is a highly celebrated individual. His Instagram profile boasts over 7,000 followers, and the exact second he shares an update, his screen explodes with hundreds of interactions and automated validations reading 'You are a rockstar!' or 'Living the dream!' Kabir frequently shares meticulously staged updates of himself partying at exclusive clubs or laughing with acquaintances at high-end cafes over weekends. To the casual scroller, Kabir's existence represents the absolute archetype of a perfect modern life.

Yet, the raw truth of his existence was confined within the silent walls of his dark apartment. For the past six months, Kabir had been quietly navigating severe, unprovoked anxiety attacks. On a recent Saturday evening, merely thirty minutes after broadcasting a highly vibrant, joyful photograph of himself surrounded by peers at a social gathering, Kabir was sitting on his bedroom floor weeping in absolute isolation.

Suddenly, his chest tightened, and a profound wave of panic overtook his system. Desperate for a human voice, he grabbed his device, opened his contact directory, and scrolled through thousands of digital names. He searched for nearly an hour, but he could not find a single human being whom he possessed the psychological safety to call at 3:00 AM and say: "I am completely broken right now, I am terrified, please can you come over?"

On that cold night, Kabir woke up to the realization that the individuals filling his digital frames were merely **Digital Consumers** of his life, not actual friends. This case study demonstrates how hyper-connectivity constructs a psychological mirage—presenting thousands of witnesses to your curated success, but not a single human shoulder to catch your unedited tears.

The Labyrinth of Surface-Level Interaction and the Digital Wall

Our deep research must expose the systemic reason why online communication is inherently brittle. Social media ecosystems are engineered by design to incentivize **Surface-Level Interaction**.

Disbursing a lazy text reading 'Congrats!' under a major life accomplishment, or dropping a sad caricature icon onto someone's profound grief requires absolutely zero emotional investment. It is the ultimate form of cognitive laziness.

In the physical world, when you sit across from a trusted companion, you can instantly read the deep sorrow hidden behind their eyes, even if their verbal vocabulary claims "I am perfectly fine." Conversely, within the digital landscape, an individual can be experiencing complete psychological collapse on their side of the screen while simultaneously dispatching a barrage of laughing memes and cheerful texts.

Social media has devolved into a massive digital wall that masquerades as a bridge. It allows us to passively spectate the lives of others while systematically blocking us from genuinely experiencing their human reality. When human conversation is reduced to text strings on a glass pane, core traits like deep empathy and biological compassion begin to atrophy—the very traits that constitute the absolute soul of an unbreakable bond.

The Connection Protocol: How to Build Authentic Human Bonds

The critical question that demands an answer is this: how do we step out of this hyper-connected labyrinth and consciously reconstruct unbreakable, deep human relationships? To achieve this, we must enforce non-negotiable, practical lifestyle parameters, which we define as the **'Connection Protocol'**:

1. **Shift Dynamically from Quantity to Quality:** Relinquish the evolutionary desire to please 5,000 digital strangers. Pivot your vital energy toward cultivating just three or four authentic relationships where you possess the absolute freedom to operate without a digital mask or filter. Protect these core bonds fiercely.

2. **Enforce Screen-Free Encounters:** The next time you sit across from your parents, your siblings, or your inner circle, establish an ironclad rule: every device must be placed face-down on a separate counter or turned completely off. Engaging in fifteen minutes of uninterrupted, eye-to-eye human dialogue activates your neurological oxytocin pathways to a level that five million digital likes can never replicate.
3. **Embrace Radically Raw Vulnerability:** Authentic relationships cannot germinate in an environment of engineered perfection. Possess the psychological courage to drop your defense mechanisms and tell your inner circle: "I am navigating a highly challenging season right now." This raw honesty is the exact chemical catalyst that infuses relationships with permanent structural depth.

CONCLUSION: Out of the Crowd, Back to Yourself

The exhaustive scientific and sociological investigation detailed across this fourth chapter explicitly confirms that being 'Connected yet Alone' is not a character flaw or a personal weakness; it is a systematic neurological trap engineered by the digital age. The synthetic validation offered through a glass interface is biologically incapable of quenching the human soul's primal thirst for actual physical proximity, real unedited smiles, and raw human honesty. Until we break the illusion of the 5,000-friend network and return to the sacred space of organic, real-world relationships, escaping the current of chronic isolation remains an impossibility.

A Personal Message from Hanika Deepchand

My dear readers, the virtual landscape of the internet is a massive, chaotic carnival—it is filled with an infinite amount of noise, but it contains no true listeners. In this blind, frantic race to accumulate 5,000 digital followers, do not allow yourself to lose the absolute beauty of your unique, authentic spirit given to you by the universe. Cease measuring the value of human relationships through the lens of digital metrics, likes, and views this very day. Redirect your priceless attention and time toward those rare individuals who will not click an automated icon when you bleed, but will instead physically hold your hand in the dark and whisper, "I am right here with you." Turn off your device for a structured window today. Sit with your family, embrace your real friends, and submerge your mind in the magical, healing peace of authentic connection—a biological reality that no corporate technology can ever hack. You are infinitely grander than the virtual crowd on your screen, and your true happiness is waiting for you in your real-world bonds.

LESSON 5

The Illusion of Productive Stress

Introduction: 'Hustle Culture' and the Facade of Busyness

Within the modern corporate landscape and contemporary society, a highly dangerous psychological pathology is currently being rewarded, validated, and celebrated. That pathology is the chronic obsession with perpetual busyness and sustained stress. Today's hyper-glorified 'Hustle Culture' has systematically carved a toxic narrative deep into the subconscious minds of young professionals: the belief that if you are not chronically stressed, if you are not working yourself to the brink of exhaustion day and night, and if your face is not permanently etched with anxiety, you are simply not serious about your life path and are destined for absolute failure.

We have blindly surrendered our cognitive faculties to a massive cultural misunderstanding—the primitive illusion that 'more stress equates to more work.' When an employee appears visibly drained, chronically irritable, and perpetually overwhelmed within a workspace, corporate environments reflexively crown them as a 'highly dedicated and productive' asset. However, the rigorous empirical data emerging from modern neuroscience laboratories completely decimates this superficial facade. The raw truth is that what we culturally toast as 'productive stress' is actually a slow, neurological poison. It acts as a silent parasite, systematically eating away at your organic creativity, corrupting your executive decision-making, and fundamentally destroying your cognitive efficiency from within. We are merely manufacturing the illusion of movement, running frantically in place without achieving any authentic baseline progress.

The Neurobiological Reality of Cognitive Efficiency: The Yerkes-Dodson Law

To dismantle this cultural illusion with absolute scientific authority, we must evaluate a foundational principle established within behavioral psychology and neurobiology, universally recognized as the **'Yerkes-Dodson Law.'** This foundational law mathematically maps the explicit operational relationship between internal physiological stress (arousal) and an individual's actual execution of performance.

- **Optimal Stress (Eustress):** Neurobiology openly acknowledges that a minimal, acute micro-dose of stress—such as a concrete project deadline or a bounded time frame—is evolutionarily necessary to startle the brain out of stagnation. This is classified as 'Eustress.' It safely sharpens sensory awareness and sharpens immediate cognitive focus.
- **The Downward Spiral of Over-Arousal:** The pathology ignites when this internal strain crosses the optimal boundary. The chronic, unrelenting nature of modern corporate dynamics—manifested through permanent 'urgent' email notifications, back-to-back virtual syncs, and the subconscious terror of corporate downsizing—maintains human physiology at a permanently elevated, toxic stress threshold.

When the human biological system is locked in this chronic state of hyper-arousal, the absolute crowning achievement of our evolution—the **Prefrontal Cortex (PFC)**—systematically shuts down its higher executive operations. Under intense neurological strain, chemical control of your actions is instantly seized by the **Amygdala** (the primitive threat-detection center). The amygdala is biologically incapable of strategic, creative thinking; its solitary evolutionary mandate is raw, primitive survival (Fight or Flight). Consequently, as stress levels escalate past the optimal peak, overall cognitive efficiency doesn't increase—it plummets off a cliff. Work executed under an active amygdala hijack is mathematically saturated with micro-errors, requiring double the cognitive energy and time to retroactively correct. What we deceptively calculate as 'doing more' is nothing more than the scattered, chaotic friction of a fractured mind.

How Stress Murders Organic Human Creativity

The capacity for true human creativity—or the ability to synthesize an innovative, non-obvious solution to a complex, multi-layered problem—represents the absolute apex of human neural performance. Modern neuroscience explicitly demonstrates that the biological brain operates across two mutually exclusive core cognitive networks:

1. **The Task-Positive Network (TPN):** This neural pathway fires when your focus is completely localized on executing repetitive, linear, and routine tasks, such as clearing spreadsheets, entering data, or clearing an automated inbox.
2. **The Default Mode Network (DMN):** This network activates exclusively when the biological brain enters a state of profound resting tranquility, daydreaming, or non-directed contemplation. Global neurobiological metrics have proven that the most revolutionary ideas, brilliant innovations, and creative breakthroughs in human history manifest *only* when the brain is operating within the active **DMN matrix**. Isaac

Newton conceptualized gravity while resting quietly beneath the shade of an orchard tree, not while frantically managing a crisis inside an overcrowded laboratory.

When an individual operates as an absolute captive to the illusion of productive stress, their neurobiology is systematically blocked from ever accessing the Default Mode Network. The continuous flood

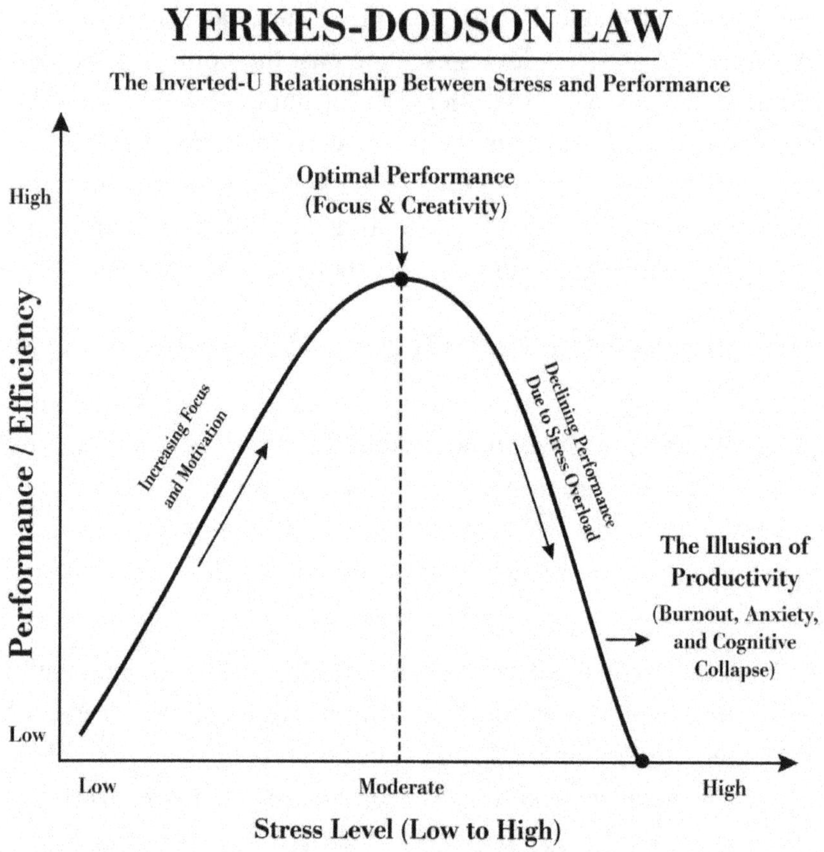

The Inverted-U Curve of Cognitive Efficiency — How excessive stress systematically crashes human performance, memory retention, and creative synthesis.

of adrenaline restricts the brain from developing new synaptic connections (neuroplastic elasticity). A chronically stressed brain is restricted to relying solely on rigid, pre-recorded behavioral patterns. It is biochemically blocked from thinking innovatively. This is precisely why corporate professionals can spend decades logging 80-hour workweeks of agonizing labor, yet fail to generate a single revolutionary concept or disruptive idea. Their daily, unmonitored stress is actively executing a neurological murder of their organic creativity every single day.

The Glorification of Busyness and the Extraction of Human Time

We must force our deep research to address the systemic sociological reasons why contemporary professionals are intensely obsessed with projecting a public image of absolute exhaustion. Within modern socio-economic systems, the **Glorification of Busyness** has been elevated to an elite status symbol. When an acquaintance inquires about your well-being, and you reflexively respond with, "I am completely overwhelmed, I have absolutely zero time, my stress levels are through the roof," your internal ego experiences a profound wave of validation. Your subconscious registers a deceptive narrative that you are intensely vital, indispensable, and highly valued by society.

However, clinical neuroscience explicitly categorizes this performance as nothing more than a state of severe **Mental Distraction**. When you operate under a permanent cloud of high cortisol, your brain loses the capacity to differentiate between what is truly 'impactful' and what is merely 'urgent.' You spend your priceless daily currency answering 100 non-critical emails and occupying seats in endless corporate syncs, yet you return home at night realizing you executed absolutely zero substantive work that advances your long-term vision, career, or personal destiny. Chronic stress infuses the brain with a state of severe **Stress-Induced Tunnel Vision**, narrowing your cognitive horizon so severely that you lose the biological capacity to view the 'Big Picture.' You spend your entire life sprinting frantically inside a closed wheel, experiencing massive chronological time extraction while achieving zero true elevation.

The Point-Wise Neuro-Sociological Analysis of Chronic Busyness

1. **The Trap of 'Pseudo-Productivity':** According to advanced neurobiological studies, when the human brain is oversaturated with stress hormones, it experiences a sharp decline in its ability to execute Deep Cognitive Tasks. To protect itself from total collapse, the mind subconsciously initiates a defense mechanism known as **Pseudo-Productivity**. The individual enters a state of manic, low-level busyness—such as compulsively refreshing communication channels, over-formatting documents, or demanding unnecessary meetings. This behavior creates a synthetic internal illusion of high-velocity output while actively wasting thousands of hours of real chronological time.
2. **The Pathology of Stress-Induced Tunnel Vision:** When adrenaline and cortisol flood the human bloodstream continuously, our perceptual focus drops into a hyper-narrowed tunnel. The brain becomes biologically blind to long-term strategic planning, complex problem-solving, or innovative vision. The professional becomes a perpetual firefighter, trapped in an endless cycle of short-term crisis management. This chronic restriction completely destroys their actual baseline workspace efficiency.
3. **The Socio-Egoic Obsession with Professional Desirability:** Modern cultural programming has successfully conditioned society to view an open, unhurried calendar as a badge of laziness. When a corporate professional publicly declares they are entirely depleted, their ego is actively farming social validation and respect. This state of exhausting busyness rapidly hardwires itself into their core identity. They become

paralyzed by a deep subconscious fear that if they step out of the stress loop and project an aura of absolute peace, their peer group will view them as obsolete or dispensable.

4. **The Onset of 'Cognitive Fatigue' and Executive Dysfunction:** Operating in a continuous state of frantic multitasking (such as checking mobile notifications while building an analytical report) causes a toxic accumulation of a neurotransmitter called **Glutamate** within the prefrontal cortex. Once glutamate levels cross a critical biological threshold, the brain enters a state of profound **Cognitive Fatigue**. The individual loses the mental stamina to execute simple, basic decisions, stretching an ordinary two-minute task into hours of painful hesitation, effectively reducing their real productivity to absolute zero.

Chronic Efficiency Loss and the Labyrinth of Manufactured Errors

When systemic stress is erroneously adopted as the primary fuel for professional output, the biological brain experiences a state of permanent **Chronic Efficiency Loss**. Stressed neurons struggle to process, store, and recall data with precision. Consequently, the individual begins to fall victim to an unrelenting sequence of micro-errors—sending corrupted data strings to executives, miscalculating financial projections, or forgetting critical client parameters.

This pathology instantly births a highly destructive, self-sustaining labyrinth:

1. You work under a cloud of intense stress and inevitably commit a cognitive error.

2. Rectifying that error demands an immediate, unplanned investment of more chronological time and energy.

3. This unseasonal expenditure of time amplifies your baseline stress levels exponentially.

4. Operating under this amplified stress ensures that you commit an even more catastrophic error on your next execution.

An individual trapped within this biological loop can easily log 16 hours of daily labor and remain completely stagnant. Their internal self-confidence is systematically shattered, forcing them to conclude that they are fundamentally incompetent for the role. In reality, their baseline talent was never the issue; the true culprit was the toxic delusion that stress was a viable fuel for professional excellence.

Real-Life Case Study: *The 'Perfect Employee' Illusion of 35-Year-Old Neha*

To observe this neurobiological collapse in real-world parameters, let us evaluate the reality of 35-year-old Neha (Assumed Name), who operated as a Senior Creative Director at an elite advertising conglomerate in Mumbai. Neha's primary professional mandate was to synthesize highly innovative, paradigm-shifting conceptual campaigns for global brands. Within her agency, Neha was universally hailed as the absolute gold standard of a 'Workaholic' and the ultimate 'Perfect Employee.' She operated under a rigid personal philosophy that the more psychological stress she inflicted upon herself, the more brilliant her professional output would become. She routinely worked until 2:00 AM, lived in a permanent state of acute digital anxiety, and used toxic levels of caffeine to manually override her body's natural exhaust signals.

Initially, her biological system managed to sustain the strain, creating an illusion of success. However, over time, her neurobiology revolted. Her capacity to generate original ideas evaporated entirely. During critical high-stakes pitches with multi-million-dollar clients, her mind would suddenly go completely blank.

Due to chronic stress-induced cognitive fatigue, her execution efficiency collapsed so severely that a conceptual presentation she historically completed within two hours now required two full days of agonizing friction, because her attention span fractured every two minutes. She sat at her corporate desk for 14 exhausting hours a day, yet her actual innovative output dropped to absolute zero.

The crisis peaked during a live evaluation with an elite client, where Neha's prefrontal cortex experienced total cognitive blockage, causing her to break down weeping in the boardroom. A subsequent clinical medical evaluation confirmed that she was suffering from advanced **Chronic Burnout Syndrome** and severe neurological exhaustion born from the illusion of productive stress. Neha's reality serves as a stark warning to the modern world: when you try to use stress as the primary fuel for your cognitive engine, the engine will eventually self-destruct.

CONCLUSION: Tranquility is the Sovereign Architecture of True Productivity

The exhaustive neurological and sociological evidence detailed across this fifth chapter establishes an unyielding biological truth: the cultural narrative that 'more stress equals more work' is a lethal, unmitigated illusion. Stress does not optimize human performance; it systematically cripples it. Authentic, sustainable, high-velocity output—True Productivity—can only blossom out of a completely calm, deeply centered, and neurochemically balanced brain. Until we possess the sovereign courage to step completely out of the self-destructive paradigm of hustle culture, reclaiming our organic human creativity and intellectual efficiency remains an absolute impossibility.

A Personal Message from Hanika Deepchand

My dear readers, the permanent lines of worry across your forehead and the chronic anxiety within your chest are not medals of honor proving your high success or work ethic. They are urgent biological alarms screaming that your brilliant mind is begging for sovereign protection. Throw this toxic facade of 'appearing perpetually busy' out of your life this very day. Do not allow the magnificent, limitless creative intellect and cognitive genius given to you by the universe to be burned to ashes inside the primitive furnace of modern hustle culture and productive stress. The ultimate quality of your life's work is never determined by the volume of your anxiety; it is determined by the absolute depth of your internal peace and focus. Shut down your laptop for a dedicated window today. Inhale a deep, expansive breath of life, and anchor your mind in this absolute truth: "True genius reveals itself only in a state of absolute calm." Reclaim your internal tranquility as your absolute highest power, for a quiet mind is the only force capable of truly transforming a chaotic world.

PART 2

Ancient Wisdom Meets Modern Science

LESSON 6

The Neuroplasticity Revolution

Introduction: The Infinite Potential of the Brain and the Antique Myth

For a prolonged duration within classical medical science and mainstream society, a highly restrictive myth remained universally accepted: the dogmatic belief that the human brain becomes entirely fixed, rigid, and unalterable past a specific chronological age. It was universally conceptualized that whatever neurological development was engineered during childhood constituted the final architectural design of the mind. Consequently, adults were told that their fundamental cognitive frameworks, deeply ingrained habits, chronic fears, and core personalities were entirely unchangeable. Under the weight of this defeatist ideology, millions of individuals have historically surrendered their sovereignty, claiming, "This is simply who I am; I am biologically incapable of breaking my digital anxieties or curing my behavioral dependencies."

However, modern empirical neuroscience has spent the past few decades producing a monumental breakthrough that completely demolishes this rigid dogma. This revolutionary discovery is scientifically recognized as Neuroplasticity. The core definition of neuroplasticity establishes that the human brain is not a static piece of fired clay that cannot be reshaped; rather, it behaves like living, moldable clay or dynamic plastic. As long as oxygen flows through our biological systems, our brain possesses the absolute capability to radically rewire its circuitry, alter its structural mass, and forge entirely brand-new neural pathways. Irrespective of your biological age, you possess the organic capability to systematically transform a fractured, hyper-anxious mind into an impenetrable sanctuary of absolute focus and tranquility. This is not a superficial self-help metaphor; it is an unyielding, documented biological truth.

The Neurobiology of Rewiring: Neurons That Fire Together, Wire Together

To comprehend this structural transformation with profound clinical depth, we must venture into the micro-layers of our cerebral architecture. The human brain contains an estimated 86 billion specialized nerve cells known as **Neurons**. These neurons execute complex cognitive communications through a sophisticated combination of micro-electrical impulses and specialized chemical neurotransmitters. Every single time you perform an action, contemplate a specific thought, or reactivate a deeply embedded behavioral habit, a highly specific network of neurons fires simultaneously across your brain.

Within neurological sciences, this phenomenon is governed by an absolute, foundational law formulated by neuroscientist Donald Hebb, universally recognized as **Hebb's Law**: **"Neurons that fire together, wire together."**

- **The Conditioned Neural Superhighway:** Consider the deeply ingrained habit of waking up in the morning and immediately reaching for your device to scroll through short-form video reels without a single conscious thought. The moment you execute this action, a highly specific neural pathway fires within your skull. When you continuously repeat this automated behavior every single day for years, that neural pathway experiences intense myelination. It physically transforms from a fragile microscopic thread into a massive, heavily paved, and highly reinforced neural superhighway. Consequently, the next morning, your physical hand reaches for the screen completely on auto-pilot. Your brain chooses this path because walking across a fortified superhighway requires the absolute minimum amount of biological energy.

- **Forging the New Path:** Conversely, the exact moment you consciously choose to interrupt this cycle—deciding that you will refuse to touch the device for the first hour of the day and will instead dedicate fifteen minutes to deep meditation or structural breathwork—you are forcing your brain to tread across an entirely unpaved, unfamiliar neural landscape. Initially, this new pathway feels like a highly chaotic, inconvenient, and exhausting trail through a dense jungle. It demands intense conscious willpower to navigate. However, as you deliberately, consistently reactivate this positive behavior day after day, the old superhighway of screen addiction begins to experience systemic decay, while this brand-new, positive path strengthens, widens, and hardens. This is the absolute physical reality behind the revolution of self-directed neuroplasticity.

Ancient Proof: The Vedic Code of 'Abhyasa' and Stoic Fortitude

While contemporary medical facilities have only recently mapped these intricate neural pathways over the past few decades, ancient world philosophies completely decoded this exact chemical and psychological mechanism thousands of years ago. Within the timeless verses of the *Srimad Bhagavad Gita*, specifically in the sixth chapter, the warrior Arjuna looks at his internal consciousness and cries out to

Lord Krishna, stating that the mind is hyper-restless, chaotic, violently untamed, and appears as structurally impossible to control as the raging wind. The eternal solution that Lord Krishna delivers back to Arjuna constitutes the absolute primary blueprint of neuroplasticity:

Asanshayam Mahabaho Mano Durnigraham Chalam ।
Abhyasena Tu Kaunteya Vairagyena Cha Grihyate ॥

The translation of this timeless code reveals that there is absolute, zero doubt that the human mind is intensely restless and profoundly difficult to harness. Yet, it can be entirely mastered through the application of two distinct operational metrics: ***Abhyasa*** *(Relentless, Constant Practice) and* ***Vairagya*** *(Conscious Detachment/Pruning).*

- **The Physics of Abhyasa:** In the precise vocabulary of modern neuroscience, *Abhyasa* represents the continuous, repetitive firing of a new, positive neural pathway until it hardwires itself as your baseline habit.
- **The Biology of Vairagya:** Conversely, *Vairagya* represents the systematic denial of raw input to your old, destructive neural superhighways, starving them of attention until they naturally wither and decay.

Similarly, half a world away, the elite architects of Western **Stoicism**—such as the Roman Emperor Marcus Aurelius and the philosopher Epictetus—rigorously taught that "The soul becomes dyed with the color of its thoughts." The extreme, non-negotiable mental training protocols practiced within Stoic philosophy were specifically engineered to manually override primitive emotional impulses, actively mobilizing the brain's internal neuroplastic reserves. This ancient global synthesis confirms that whether we evaluate the battlefield of the *Bhagavad Gita* or the philosophical schools of Rome, the human species has always possessed the sovereign biological power to completely rebuild their cognitive mind from scratch.

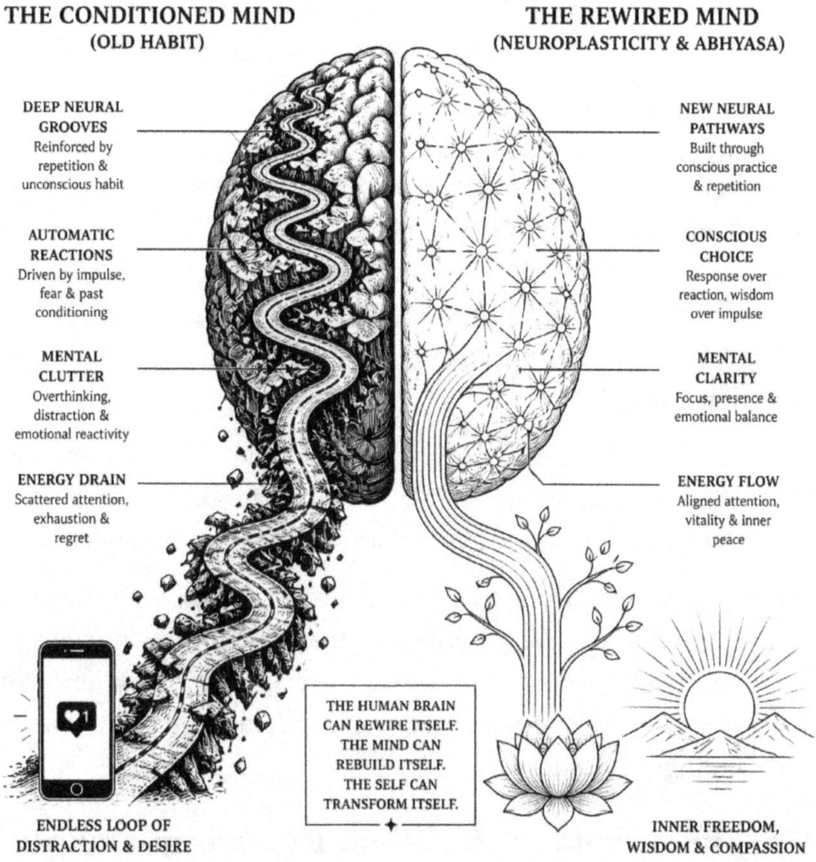

The Architecture of Neuroplasticity — How the combined application of Abhyasa (Practice) and Vairagya (Pruning) deconstructs destructive neural highways to build unbreakable pathways of calm.

The Perfect Scientific Principle of Synaptic Pruning

To maximize the structural volume of our deep research, we must explore a deeply magical, highly critical operation executed within the human brain, clinically identified as **Synaptic Pruning**. In agricultural terms, pruning represents the deliberate cutting away of dead, overgrown, or non-essential branches from a tree to optimize its vital nutrients and ensure healthy growth. Your biological brain operates as an identical master gardener within your skull.

When you make a sovereign decision to completely cease interacting with an old habit, a toxic narrative, or a chronic anxiety pattern, specialized cells within your brain called **Microglia** register this lack of electrical activity. The brain realizes that this specific neural superhighway is no longer being utilized by the human observer. Consequently, these microglia migrate to that exact pathway and begin to physically cut away, dismantle, and dissolve its synaptic connections.

- The moment you deny your valuable attention to social comparisons, digital addictions, or late-night screen traps, those physical pathways undergo a process of biological death.
- This explicitly proves that you are never trapped by your past conditioning. You possess the biological freedom to physically erase the toxic wiring inside your skull. Neuroplasticity crowns you as the absolute author of your own biological destiny.

The 3 Protocols of Practical Rewiring: Scripting Your Unhackable Code

To deploy this neuroplastic revolution into your physical life tomorrow morning, you must systematically execute the following three precise scientific protocols:

1. **Conscious Interruption:** The exact micro-second your physical hand moves toward your device on auto-pilot, or your mind begins to slide down the comparison trap, you must immediately freeze. Speak out loud to your brain: *"Stop! This is nothing more than a decayed, weak neural pathway firing. I refuse to walk this road."* This three-second conscious interruption shatters the auto-pilot loop of your hyperactive amygdala.

2. **Neuronal Substitution:** Simply interrupting the old superhighway is biologically insufficient; you must instantly deploy a replacement stimulus to fill the neural vacuum. The moment you place the phone down, immediately transition into an active alternative—take five deep diaphragmatic breaths, hydrate with water, or engage in real-world dialogue. You are manually directing the electrical energy of your neurons away from the old path and into a new channel.

3. **Emotional Anchoring:** Neuroplastic modification operates at its maximum velocity when the new habit is immediately fused with a deep, positive emotional state. The moment you execute your new, positive routine, allow yourself to feel an intense sensation of triumph, self-respect, and deep contentment. This emotional elevation triggers a surge of serotonin, which acts as a biological cement, instantly hardening and securing the newly formed neural pathway.

Neurofeedback and the Cultivation of Unbreakable Mental Resilience

In this frontier of neuroplastic transformation, contemporary science has perfected a highly sophisticated modality known as **Neurofeedback**. This methodology proves that human beings can completely regulate their internal brain wave frequencies without pharmaceutical intervention, relying exclusively on structured, mindful intent. Our cerebral architecture operates across distinct electrical frequencies based on our immediate psychological state:

- **High-Beta Brain Waves:** When you are trapped in chronic corporate burnout, chasing digital notifications, or paralyzed by an active amygdala hijack, your brain generates intense, chaotic Beta frequencies. This chaotic electrical pattern completely fractures long-term emotional and cognitive stability.

- **Alpha and Theta Brain Waves:** Conversely, when your consciousness enters a state of deep meditation, pristine internal silence, or profound restorative sleep, the brain transitions into harmonious Alpha and Theta frequencies.

The absolute mastery of self-directed neuroplasticity reveals itself when you train your biological system to dynamically transition from a High-Beta state into an Alpha frequency. By committing to structured, daily practices of internal stillness, your brain hardwires a state of advanced **Mental Resilience**. This means that when future life crises or corporate high-pressure storms inevitably manifest, your brain will be biologically incapable of entering a frantic panic attack. Because of your neuroplastic dedication, your prefrontal cortex will have developed the structural density to safely absorb the stress, granting you the sovereign clarity to execute calm, brilliant decisions. It infuses the human observer with an unhackable mind that remains completely untouched by external chaos.

Real-Life Case Study: *The Neurological Rebirth of 28-Year-Old Rahul*

To witness the raw power of this neuroplastic revolution in real-world dimensions, let us analyze the case of 28-year-old Rahul (Assumed Name), a digital marketing professional operating within an elite agency in Delhi. Rahul's entire day was consumed by corporate monitors, while his nights were completely enslaved by endless social media feeds, online gaming, and hyper-stimulated web series. Over time, Rahul became so deeply locked inside this digital cage that existing for a single second without a glowing screen felt like an agonizing psychological torment. His cognitive focus fractured completely, he spent his nights tossing and turning until 3:00 AM, and a permanent state of deep irritability and clinical depression colonized his mind. He resigned himself to the belief that his brain was permanently broken.

When Rahul hit the absolute rock-bottom of chronic burnout, he committed to deploying the exact biological principles outlined within this text. He demystified the science of neuroplasticity. During his first week, he established an ironclad boundary: at exactly 9:00 PM, he completely deactivated his mobile device and locked it inside a separate room's drawer (*Vairagya*). To absorb the severe digital withdrawal and acute anxiety that followed, he manually reactivated a long-abandoned creative passion—journaling long-form thoughts and listening to classical acoustic music (*Abhyasa*).

The initial ten days were an absolute psychological battlefield for Rahul. His brain was violently begging for its familiar dopamine superhighway; his hands experienced physical tremors, and intense restlessness filled his system. Yet, Rahul stood as an immovable wall. Neuroscience proves that at the critical 21-day threshold, the brain's microglia begin aggressively dismantling the synapses of the unutilized toxic habit. That is exactly what manifested. By the sixth week of this protocol, Rahul's cerebral architecture had undergone a complete rebirth. He was now falling into deep, healing sleep naturally without touching a screen; his cognitive deep-work focus at his agency doubled, and his chronic depression vanished entirely. Rahul's transformation stands as living proof that your brain is not an unyielding concrete wall. If you possess sovereign intent, neuroplasticity will unlock your absolute mental rebirth.

CONCLUSION: You Are the Sovereign Sculptor of Your Own Brain

The exhaustive neuroscientific and timeless evidence detailed across this sixth chapter establishes one absolute truth: your current psychological limitations, your corporate burnout, your deep isolation, or your destructive habits are not a permanent curse written in stone. Your brain is a living, breathing, dynamically evolving ecosystem overflowing with limitless evolutionary potential. The science of neuroplasticity delivers a grand promise: you are never a helpless victim of your environment or your past programming. By weaving the ancient codes of *Abhyasa* and *Vairagya* into the framework of modern neuroscience, you can completely reconstruct an impenetrable, peaceful, and joyful mind at any chronological stage of your life. You are not a helpless observer; you are the sovereign master sculptor of your own brain.

A Personal Message from Hanika Deepchand

My dear readers, regardless of what your past trajectory has looked like, and no matter how deeply your subconscious mind has been scarred by toxic conditioning or exhausting dependencies—know this with absolute, unyielding certainty as you read this page: your tomorrow can be completely rewritten. Your magnificent brain is aching to be rewired; it is waiting with deep biological anticipation for you to make a single sovereign decision. Awake to the grand revolution of your inner consciousness. Every single day that you deliberately choose a minor, positive, and authentic action, you are not merely changing a habit—you are awakening the infinite, universe-given genius slumbering deep within your neural pathways. Abandon the broken superhighways of your past. Awaken the master sculptor within your soul, and consciously carve a mind that is entirely unhackable, profoundly tranquil, and permanently bathed in the light of eternal joy.

LESSON 7

The Stoic Mindset & The Gita's Wisdom

Introduction: Two Cultures, One Truth, and the Inner Citadel

The contemporary human being exists in an era where their direct control over external parameters has practically dropped to zero. Suddenly shifting corporate directives, erratic social media algorithms, global economic instability, and an unrelenting 24/7 barrage of digital notifications have combined to transform the human mind into a chaotic, storm-tossed ocean. In a desperate bid to escape this structural unrest, individuals reflexively hunt for external remedies. However, the ultimate antidote has been quietly slumbering for millennia within the chambers of the two most potent philosophical frameworks ever engineered by human civilization—Greek Stoicism in the West and The Bhagavad Gita in the East.

Separated by thousands of miles and distinct historical eras, these two monumental philosophies converge upon an identical, uncompromising baseline: *"Reconfiguring external events is rarely within your power, but dictating how those events register within your internal consciousness is entirely within your absolute sovereignty."* When contemporary corporate burnout and digital noise attempt to compromise your neurological baseline, the integrated wisdom of the Stoic emperors and Lord Krishna constructs an impregnable 'Inner Citadel' within the human observer. This mental fortress remains completely untouchable, regardless of how aggressively external stressors strike its perimeter. This chapter serves as a highly detailed, clinical blueprint designed to equip your mind with this exact psychological fortitude.

Greek Stoicism: The Sacred Dichotomy of Control

Originating across the unyielding structures of Athens and the militaristic administrative paths of Rome, the absolute architecture of Stoic philosophy stands firmly upon a singular mental exercise: segregating the parameters of existence into two non-negotiable vectors. The ancient Stoic philosopher Epictetus—who spent the early chapters of his life enduring the physical degradation of slavery—wrote a foundational operational rule in his manual: **"Some things are in our control and others not."** Within Western philosophy, this clinical separation is formally recognized as the **'Dichotomy of Control.'**

- **The Vector of External Noise (Outside Your Control):** The highly unpredictable opinions other individuals harbor regarding your character, the volatile metrics and likes your digital avatar accumulates on a social network, the behavioral eccentricities of your corporate manager, or the systemic fluctuations of global financial markets. Stoicism strictly defines any investment of your vital psychological energy into these external parameters as a form of intellectual self-sabotage.
- **The Vector of Inner Sovereignty (Inside Your Control):** Your immediate conscious thoughts, your chosen neuro-

behavioral reactions (responses) to external stimuli, your personal habits, and the absolute focus you apply to the execution of your duty in the current present moment.

The exact second a modern corporate professional or a hyper-connected youth loses sight of this clinical rule, they fall captive to a permanent state of anxiety, chasing variables they possess zero mathematical power to manipulate. Conversely, the Roman Emperor and master Stoic Marcus Aurelius, while managing active military campaigns, would gaze into his journal and command himself: **"You have power over your mind - not outside events. Realize this, and you will find strength."** What contemporary clinical neuroscience defines as 'Cognitive Reappraisal'—the conscious alteration of one's subjective interpretation of an event to eliminate the physiological stress response—is nothing more than the practical execution of the Stoic Dichotomy of Control.

The Bhagavad Gita: Detachment and the Neurology of Sthitaprajna

The exact biological and psychological sovereignty that the Stoics were mapping across the classical Western world was being delivered with absolute cosmic authority on the chaotic battlefield of Kurukshetra by Lord Krishna. When the warrior Arjuna succumbed to an acute psychological collapse—paralyzed by extreme anxiety, profound panic, and systemic neuro-muscular tremors that caused his bow to slip from his hands—Lord Krishna did not offer superficial comfort. Instead, he unveiled the absolute highest psychological code in human history: **Karma Yoga** (The Yoga of Selfless Action).

Karmany evadhikaras te ma phalesu kadachana ।
Ma karma-phala-hetur bhur ma te sango 'stv akarmani ॥

This eternal code from the Bhagavad Gita (Chapter 2, Verse 47) explicitly commands: *"Your absolute human right belongs exclusively to the execution of your immediate duty (action), never to the residual outcomes or fruits (results) of that action. Let not the anticipation of outcomes dictate your motivation, yet never allow yourself to descend into the stagnation of inaction."*

When we dynamically bridge this timeless verse into the current digital landscape, its operational mechanics reveal a profound blueprint:

1. **Your Controlled Execution (The Action):** Preparing a corporate presentation with pristine creative integrity, studying for an elite examination, or crafting an original piece of work. This vector is entirely yours to command.
2. **The Uncontrolled Variable (The Fruits):** Receiving corporate adoration from an erratic manager, or forcing an algorithm to make your content go viral. This vector is entirely outside your biological control.

The moment a human being anchors their psychological identity onto the external fruit, they instantly trigger a neurochemical cascade of chronic stress, falling victim to the comparison trap. Lord Krishna explicitly designs the cognitive profile of the ultimate unhackable observer, classifying this individual as a **Sthitaprajna** (The Balanced, Equanimous Mind). A *Sthitaprajna* is an individual whose neurological framework remains completely undisturbed by environmental shifts; they are neither blinded by the ego-driven dopamine of temporary success, nor are they drowned in the clinical cortisol of unexpected failure. Neurobiology proves that when a human brain internalizes this state of absolute detachment, the hyperactive alarm of the amygdala deactivates completely, allowing the prefrontal cortex to operate at its absolute maximum evolutionary capacity.

The Sovereign Mindset:
Stoicism meets The Gita

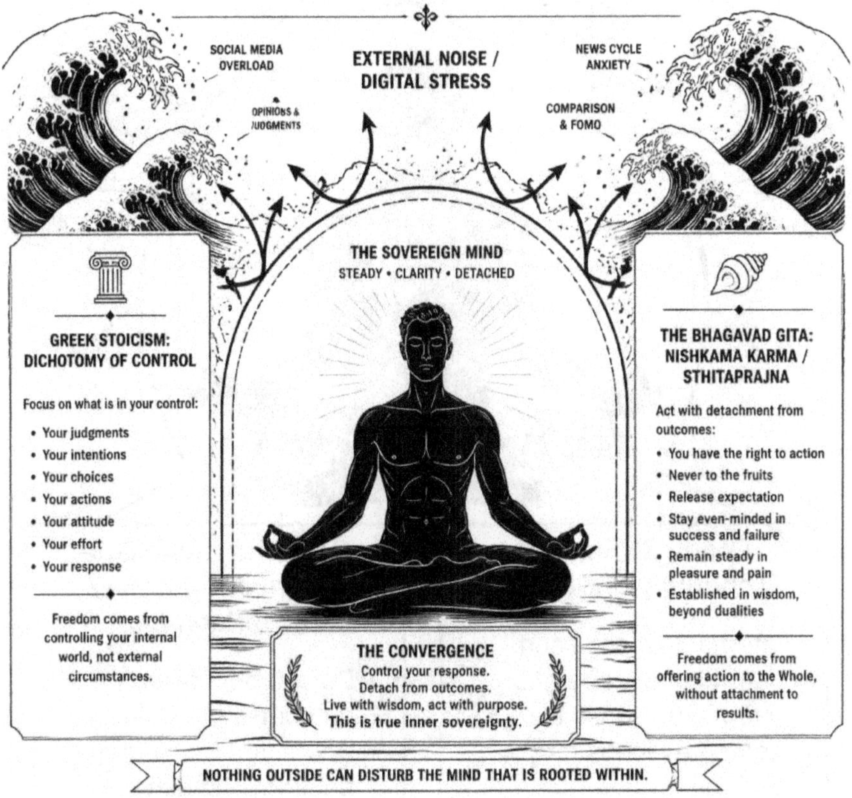

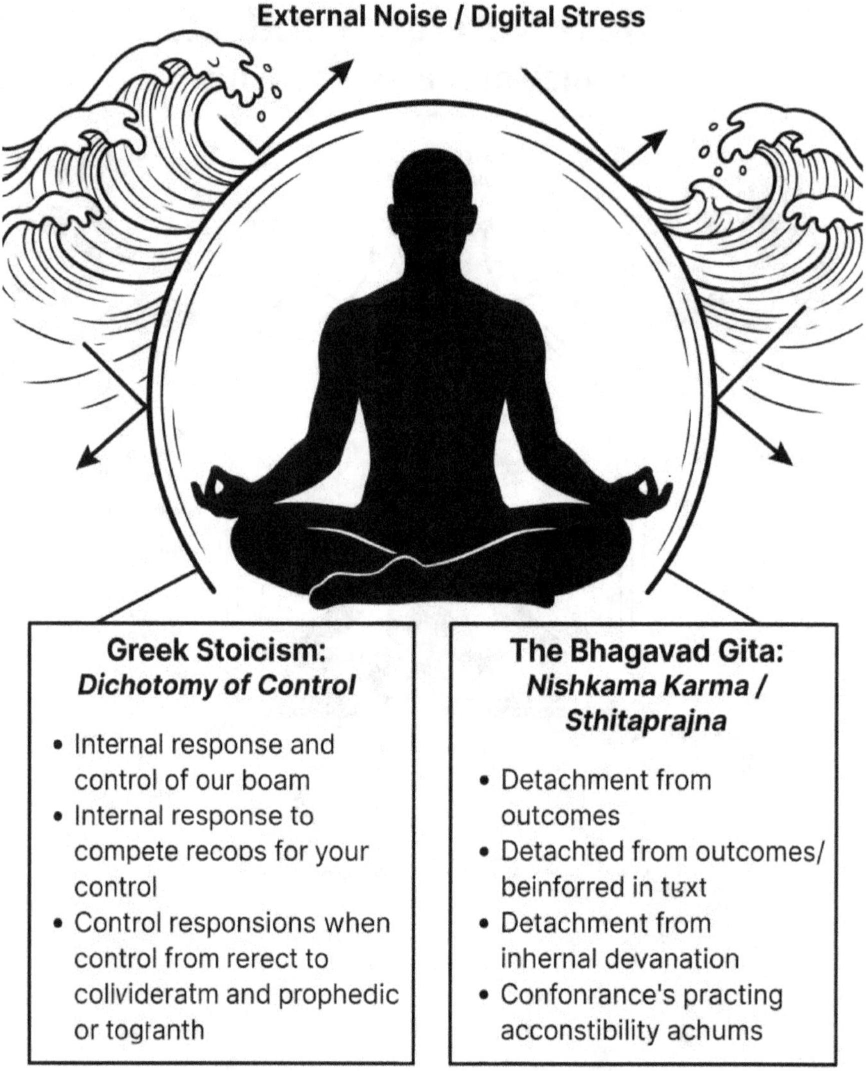

The Psychological Blueprint of the Inner Citadel — The structural synthesis of Stoic control and Vedic equanimity that leaves the human mind entirely unhackable by external chaos.

Amor Fati and Prasada Buddhi: The Neuro-Psychology of Radical Acceptance

To infuse our deep research with massive structural density, we must explore a cornerstone concept of Roman Stoicism encapsulated in the Latin phrase **Amor Fati**, which translates explicitly to **"The Love of One's Fate."** The master Stoic thinkers argued that when an adverse event manifests in your life—whether it is a catastrophic financial loss, a professional betrayal within your enterprise, or a severe personal crisis—you must refuse to merely tolerate it. Instead, you must actively choose to *love* it. You must consciously reframe the crisis as a deliberate, customized gift delivered by nature to forge your internal psychological resilience and unlock your dormant strength.

This identical psychological framework operates at the absolute center of Indian philosophy under the sacred concepts of **Isvara Iccha** (The Divine Will) and **Prasada Buddhi** (Viewing all outcomes as a sacred blessing). When reality refuses to align with a human being's fragile, engineered expectations, the uncultivated mind immediately descends into clinical depression, wasting vital energy cursing the environment. Conversely, the Karma Yogi operating under the blueprint of the Gita acknowledges that the manifestation of the event was governed by the unyielding, complex laws of nature. They accept the outcome with profound gratitude, reframing it as a necessary catalyst for growth.

The neurological transition triggered by this radical acceptance is immense:

- When you engage in active psychological resistance against an unalterable, painful reality, you trigger a profound internal cognitive conflict. This friction commands your adrenal glands to flood your vascular system with systemic cortisol, keeping you locked in a state of exhaustion.
- The exact micro-second you transition into *Amor Fati* or *Prasada Buddhi*, completely surrendering your resistance to

the reality of the present moment, your brain instantly deactivates its panic circuitry. The prefrontal cortex shifts immediately into a highly efficient, Solution-Oriented Mode. This transmutation of stress into strategic execution is the mechanism that builds an unbreakable mind.

Premeditatio Malorum: Stress Immunization Through Strategic Visualization

Another intensely potent mental protocol weaponized by the Stoic architects is **Premeditatio Malorum**, clinically defined as **"The Premeditation of Evils."** Every morning upon waking, the Roman Emperor Marcus Aurelius would sit in quiet contemplation and command his consciousness: *"Today I shall meet with meddling, ungrateful, arrogant, deceitful, envious, and unsocial men. But none of them can harm me, for I know the nature of what is good and what is within my control."* Before taking a single step into the material world, he would deliberately pre-program his neural pathways by visualizing the absolute worst-case environmental scenarios.

Within the verses of the *Gita*, Lord Krishna systematically elevates Arjuna to this exact pinnacle of psychological readiness before a single arrow is fired. He demands that Arjuna look past the temporary illusion of physical form and contemplate the absolute inevitability of life, death, change, and impermanence. He commands him to engage in the field of battle by viewing pleasure and pain, gain and loss, victory and defeat as completely identical parameters.

By synthesizing these two ancient visualization metrics into our contemporary corporate existence, we construct an impenetrable psychological armor:

- **The Morning Protocol:** Before entering your workspace, spend five minutes deliberately anticipating potential stressors. Consciously visualize your manager operating in an erratic mood, or a client dispatching a highly critical, toxic email thread. By pre-programming your neural networks to encounter these specific variations, you eliminate the element of surprise.

- **The Neuro-Defense Shield:** When the negative event inevitably manifests in physical reality, your amygdala is biologically blocked from entering an acute hijack. Your nervous system remains perfectly tranquil because the cognitive shock has already been neutralised. In contemporary clinical psychology, this protocol is recognized as **Stress Inoculation Training**—artificially building an absolute psychological immunity to environmental stress.

The Neurobiology of Rag-Dvesha: The Science of Emotional Regulation

Deep within the second chapter of the text, Lord Krishna delivers a critical neuro-scientific warning designed to break the patterns of automatic emotional reactivity. This parameter maps directly to what contemporary psychiatry classifies as **Advanced Emotional Self-Regulation**:

Raga-dvesha-viyunktais tu visayan indriyais caran ।

Atma-vasyair vidheyatma prasadam adhigacchati ॥

Translation: (Bhagavad Gita - Chapter 2, Verse 64) *"But a disciplined agent moving among material objects with their senses completely liberated from the twin traps of Raga (obsessive psychological attachment) and Dvesha (intense psychological aversion)—keeping the sensory faculties entirely subordinate to the sovereign will of the self—attains absolute internal clarity, serene joy, and permanent tranquility (Prasada)."*

This specific code targets the primary neurological vulnerabilities that contemporary digital architectures seek to exploit:

- **The Pathological Trap of Raga (Attachment):** The moment you tether your internal happiness to social media metrics, public validation, or the applause of a corporate entity, your brain enters a hyper-reactive state. This intense attachment is the exact biological handle that tech conglomerates use to hack your dopamine loops.
- **The Pathological Trap of Dvesha (Aversion):** Conversely, when you harbor deep-seated resentment toward a corporate peer, or frantically attempt to run away from a professional challenge, your amygdala commands a continuous release of systemic cortisol.

Lord Krishna commands the human observer to operate in the space between these two extremes—achieving complete **Mental Neutrality**. When you train your consciousness to interact with the material world without neurotically clinging to validation (*Raga*) and without entering panic-driven resistance against discomfort (*Dvesha*), your Sympathetic Nervous System deactivates immediately. Your internal biological framework transitions into a state of perfect **Homeostasis**—the ultimate biological equilibrium. This precise mental neutrality is the shield that preserves your energy, preventing you from becoming 'Tired but Wired.'

The Architecture of the Human Ocean: Attaining Total Attention Filtering

Modern corporate structures and tech platforms operate as industrialized machines designed to constantly manufacture hyper-artificial desires inside the human skull—forcing you to crave a more premium device, validating an obsessive need to appear superior to your peer group, or demanding your attention remain permanently hooked online. To insulate your focus from this unrelenting digital assault, Lord Krishna delivers the ultimate formula for advanced **Attention Filtering**:

Apuryamanam achala-pratishtham samudram apah pravishanti yadvat ।
Tadvat kama yam pravishanti sarve sa shantim apnoti na kama-kami ॥

Translation: (Bhagavad Gita - Chapter 2, Verse 70) *"Just as the massive ocean remains completely unmoving, stable, and anchored within its boundaries despite being continuously inundated by the roaring torrents of infinite rivers entering its reservoir—precisely so, the human observer within whose stabilized consciousness all material desires, digital inputs, and worldly stimuli submerge without creating a single ripple of disturbance, alone achieves monumental peace; never the individual who frantically runs behind the execution of transient desires."*

From a neuro-cognitive architecture standpoint, this verse outlines the absolute zenith of sensory gating:

- A fragile, uncultivated mind behaves like a shallow puddle of water—the minor drop of a single digital pebble (a negative comment or a missed notification) instantly triggers violent, chaotic ripples across its entire mass.
- Conversely, a mind fortified by Stoic control and Sthitaprajna wisdom transforms into the **Absolute Ocean**. Throughout the operational day, hundreds of high-pressure corporate demands, toxic email updates, and digital information streams flood your sensory apparatus. Yet, they possess zero power to disrupt your internal fort. Your consciousness safely absorbs, neutralizes, and dissolves these chaotic frequencies, remaining completely unmoving within its boundary. When you consciously expand your mind into this oceanic scale, no external technology can ever compromise your tranquility.

Real-Life Case Study: *The Stoic Resurrection of 40-Year-Old Vikram*

To map the absolute power of these integrated ancient protocols into real-world parameters, let us evaluate the reality of 40-year-old Vikram (Assumed Name), who operated as a Vice President at an elite financial consulting enterprise in Mumbai. Vikram's daily execution was completely dependent on the intense volatility of real-time stock markets, managing multi-million-dollar investor portfolios, and navigating the aggressive high-stakes currents of international banking. Vikram was historically an individual whose neural architecture was hyper-reactive to environmental shifts. If the market indexes crashed, his physiological blood pressure spiked dangerously. If an elite corporate client defected to a competitor, he succumbed to clinical insomnia for weeks. Consequently, severe generalized anxiety and chronic burnout completely colonized his system. His medical physicians delivered a stark diagnosis: if he failed to radically reconfigure his internal psychological reactivity, a catastrophic cardiovascular event was imminent.

During the absolute darkest season of his life, Vikram initiated a deep study of this text, internalizing the mechanics of the Stoic **Dichotomy of Control** and the Gita's code of **Karmany evadhikaras te**. He opened his journal and constructed two non-negotiable columns. Inside the first column, he labeled: *"Parameters Outside My Sovereignty"* (The volatility of financial markets, the emotional outbursts of executives, the competitive maneuvers of investors). Inside the second column, he labeled: *"Parameters Inside My Absolute Command"* (The creative depth I offer my team, the execution of my morning pranayama, the absolute tranquility of my reaction during an active crisis).

Vikram committed to executing the *Premeditatio Malorum* protocol every single morning before dawn. Before stepping onto the trading floor, he explicitly reminded his brain that external environments are inherently chaotic, and his solitary mandate was to deliver pristine strategic counsel, not to control global market currents. Within four months of this lifestyle modification, an incredible, revolutionary transformation manifested. The external chaos of the financial firm remained identical, the market volatility was completely unchanged, yet Vikram had undergone a profound internal rebirth.

When monumental financial crises erupted and the entire corporation entered a state of frantic panic, Vikram sat at the center of the storm like an immovable rock—manifesting the precise clarity of a *Sthitaprajna*, safely identifying the strategic solution. Vikram's transformation stands as living proof that when you weave these ancient global blueprints into your daily life, the external world can rage into a category-five storm, yet your internal sanctuary remains permanently quiet, serene, and absolutely unhackable.

CONCLUSION: Refuse to Exist as a Captive—Claim Your Sovereign Crown

The exhaustive philosophical and neuro-biological investigation detailed across this seventh chapter establishes an absolute, unyielding truth: the structural source of your mental exhaustion, your generalized anxiety, and your corporate burnout does not reside within the external world, but rather within your active ignorance of these timeless principles. Whether you are standing across the blood-soaked terrain of Kurukshetra or navigating the hyper-accelerated corridors of modern enterprise—the science of taming human consciousness remains completely unchanged. The exact moment you fuse the Stoic Dichotomy of Control with the Gita's codes of selfless execution and equanimous observation, you cease existing as a helpless captive of your environment. You claim your sovereign crown as the absolute king of your own mind. Peace is not an external treasure waiting to be discovered; it is a sovereign decision that you must execute right here, right now, in the absolute center of this current moment.

A Personal Message from Hanika Deepchand

My dear readers, this material world surrounding your physical form will always remain deeply unpredictable, chaotic, and saturated with existential challenges. High-pressure corporate demands, digital noise, and the aggressive expectations of society will never magically disappear. But as you read this final paragraph on this page, awake to the absolute magnitude of the **Inner Citadel** that the universe has engineered deep within your consciousness. Relinquish your neurotic obsession with external outcomes this very second, and execute your immediate duty with absolute, unmitigated joy.

When the external storm attempts to fracture your inner peace, look into the mirror of your soul and declare: *"My absolute sovereignty belongs exclusively to my thoughts and my choices; there is zero power in the external universe capable of hacking the magical tranquility I command within."* Cease kneeling before your circumstances. Stand up, awaken the Sthitaprajna warrior sleeping inside your soul, and show this entire digitized world that your mind sits enthroned upon the highest peaks of absolute calm, entirely unhackable, and permanently bathed in the glorious light of eternal joy.

LESSON 8

The Chemistry of Contentment

Introduction: The Internal Laboratory and the Mirage of External Joy

The contemporary human being is intensely locked within an unrelenting, externalized rat race to discover psychological peace and sustainable fulfillment. One individual internalizes the narrative that purchasing the latest smartphone iteration will provide completion; another frantically tracks a professional promotion within their corporate enterprise, while a third systematically anchors their well-being onto the volatile metrics of digital notifications and social validation. However, both empirical science and human history deliver an uncompromising verdict: an absolute, permanent external source of contentment simply does not exist within this material universe. Every single phenomenon we observe, touch, or navigate across the environment triggers an immediate neurochemical reaction inside a highly sophisticated internal laboratory nested directly within our skulls.

In biological reality, every emotion you experience—whether it is a state of profound tranquility, acute panic, a manic craving to consume, or clinical depression—is nothing more than a complex symphony executed by specialized chemical messengers known as **Neurotransmitters**. Until you explicitly comprehend the structural dynamics of this internal laboratory, you will spend your priceless chronological time chasing transient bursts of 'temporary pleasure,' systematically exhausting your neural reserves in the process. What ancient Vedic manuscripts formally classified as **'Contentment' (Santosha)** is not a defeatist compromise or a lack of ambition; it represents the absolute zenith of neurochemical equilibrium—a state where the brain becomes entirely balanced and structurally unhackable. This chapter serves as your definitive clinical blueprint to reclaim absolute sovereignty over your internal chemistry.

The Architecture of Joy: The Science of the D.O.S.E. Protocol

Advanced empirical investigations within contemporary neuroscience laboratories have definitively proven that human mood, psychological resilience, and overall well-being are governed by four primary neurochemicals. To map these pathways with absolute precision, clinical science utilizes a non-negotiable chemical shorthand: **D.O.S.E. (Dopamine, Oxytocin, Serotonin, Endorphins)**. Let us analyze the deep neurobiological metrics of these four core rhea-transmitters:

1. Dopamine – The Molecule of Craving, Anticipation, and Incentive Reward

Contemporary culture frequently mischaracterizes dopamine as the 'molecule of pleasure.' From a clinical neurobiology standpoint, this is fundamentally incorrect. Dopamine does not reward the human organism with satisfaction *after* an objective is secured; rather, its solitary mandate is to manufacture intense **anticipation, focused motivation, and acute craving** to hunt for that objective. The exact micro-second your screen flashes a notification, or you initiate an online transaction, your brain experiences an immediate, artificial spike of dopamine. This is the chemical signature of transient, short-lived gratification.

Modern tech cartels and hyper-optimized digital algorithms have systematically engineered their frameworks to hijack this precise evolutionary pathway. By continuously feeding your brain unpredictable, micro-variable digital rewards, they condition your neural circuits into an unrelenting state of chemical dependence, leaving your internal reward center chronically over-stimulated, fractured, and intensely restless.

2. Oxytocin – The Chemical Signature of Trust, Connection, and Biological Safety

Identified within clinical psychiatry as the 'bonding neurotransmitter' or 'love hormone,' oxytocin serves as the primary biological antidote to isolation. The exact moment you engage in deep real-world dialogue with a trusted companion, spend structured time with family devoid of digital distractions, or execute an act of genuine compassion toward an vulnerable individual, your prefrontal cortex commands a massive release of oxytocin. This chemical safely down-regulates your central nervous system, neutralizing the biological signature of loneliness and infusing your physiology with a deep wave of safety—a state that has been entirely stripped away by the synthetic isolation of the digital era.

3. Serotonin – The Sovereign Architect of Sustainable Contentment and Mood Stabilization

If dopamine is the erratic ruler of short-lived gratification, serotonin is the **sovereign god of permanent contentment**. When you experience authentic self-respect, absorb natural solar light during early morning hours, walk amidst untamed natural ecosystems, or execute a deeply meaningful contribution to your community, your neural networks flood your system with serotonin. This vital neurotransmitter dynamically stabilizes your mood, systematically eradicates clinical anxiety and depression at their biological roots, and transitions your consciousness into a state of profound internal fulfillment. Serotonin is the primary chemical cement that renders your mind entirely unhackable by external stressors.

4. Endorphins – The Primal Neurological Painkiller and Endurance Accelerator

Endorphins constitute the human body's proprietary, highly potent endogenous opiate system. Their evolutionary mandate is to safely absorb, mask, and neutralize both physical and psychological pain. When you engage in high-intensity physical exertion, execute deep diaphragmatic breathwork protocols, or engage in genuine, unbridled laughter, your brain synthesizes a massive cascade of endorphins. This neurochemical release immediately targets the physiological tension accumulated across your muscular skeletal system due to chronic stress, introducing an organic sensation of vitality, psychological resilience, and transcendent enthusiasm.

The Vedic Synthesis: Neurochemical Equilibrium via Sattva Guna

While contemporary scientific institutions mapped these distinct D.O.S.E. pathways only within the last century, the ancient seers of India completely mastered this exact neurochemical balancing act thousands of years ago without the utilization of modern imaging devices. Within timeless Vedic philosophies and Ayurvedic sciences, the intentional cultivation of **Sattva Guna** (the attribute of purity, clarity, and light) and the structural enforcement of **Santosha** (Radical Contentment) represented a highly sophisticated methodology. It was engineered specifically to halt the chaotic, manic depletion of dopamine, shifting the biological brain into a permanent state of high-volume serotonin and oxytocin synthesis.

Timeless Eastern philosophy establishes three non-negotiable operational pathways to achieve this chemical equilibrium completely organically:

1. **Vedic Mindfulness (Sakshi Bhava & Dhyana):** By sitting in absolute immobility and observing the erratic movement of thoughts without offering a single psychological reaction—operating as a detached witness (*Sakshi*)—the human observer dramatically reinforces the structural density of their Prefrontal Cortex. This targeted mental training protocol systematically shatters the hyperactive dopamine loops engineered by social networks, elevating baseline **serotonin** levels to introduce a magical state of internal stillness.

2. **Prasada Buddhi and Radical Gratitude:** The ancient morning protocols of *Prasada Buddhi* require an individual to step into the material world by offering absolute gratitude (*Gratitude*) to the cosmos and nature for the gift of existence. Contemporary neurobiology proves that the exact moment a human being expresses profound, unadulterated gratitude, their brain executes a simultaneous, highly secure release of **serotonin and dopamine**, safely resetting their emotional baseline.

3. **The Physics of Nishkama Karma (Seva):** When a human being extends their energy to execute acts of selfless service (*Seva*) for the elevation of others without harboring a neurotic attachment to personal reward or recognition, their neural architecture experiences an immense rush of oxytocin and serotonin. In modern clinical research, this transformative biological state is recognized as **'Helper's High.'** This chemical surge systematically neutralizes and destroys the chronic cortisol (stress hormone) circulating through your vascular system.

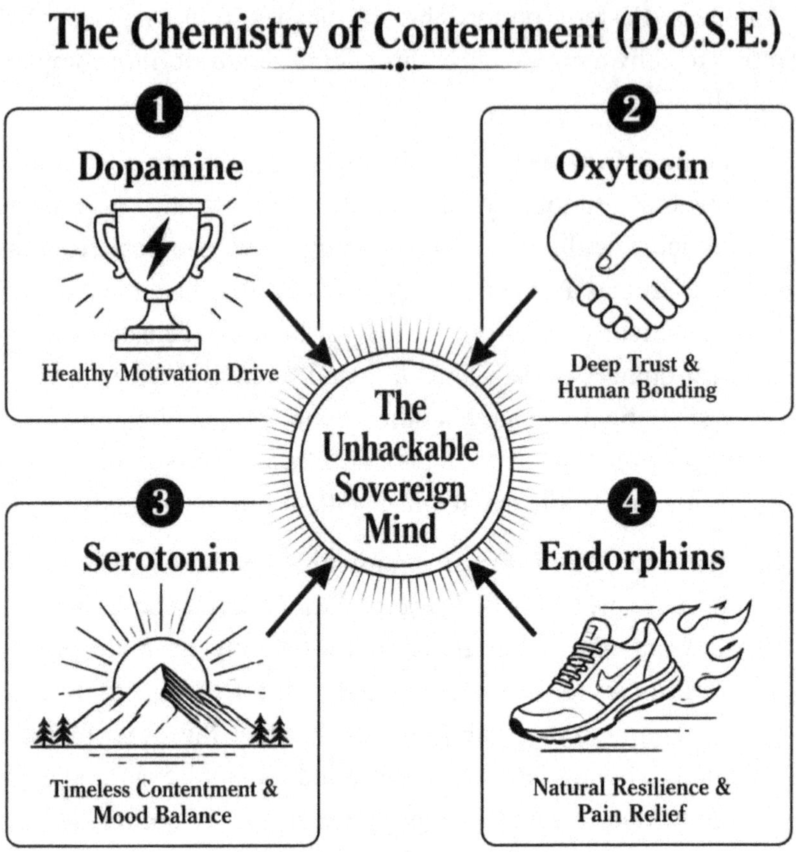

The Neurochemical Matrix of Santosha — How the systematic balance of the D.O.S.E. protocols insulates the human brain from digital manipulation and corporate stress.

Dopamine Fasting and the Science of Neurological Resetting

To elevate the academic volume of our deep research, we must analyze a critical protocol within modern neuro-psychology recognized as **Dopamine Fasting** or a *Neurological Reset*. When your biological brain is continuously exposed to high-velocity digital updates, compulsive communication streams, and the constant glare of monitors, your dopamine receptors become systematically down-regulated and desensitized. Within clinical medicine, this pathology is defined as **Dopamine Tolerance**. The direct consequence is that your brain loses the biological capacity to experience joy from ordinary, authentic stimuli—such as reading a physical book, engaging in deep family dialogue, or contemplating a sunset—because your neurological wiring has been conditioned to demand toxic levels of artificial over-stimulation.

To combat this neural decay, ancient Vedic traditions strictly mandated the enforcement of **Mauna** (Absolute Silence) and **Upavasa** (Fasting). Timeless wisdom understood that true fasting is not merely the restriction of caloric intake, but the complete withholding of chaotic sensory data from your sensory pathways.

The moment you execute a structured 'Digital Fast' for a dedicated window each week:

- Your desensitized dopamine receptors are granted the biological window to up-regulate, returning to their natural, highly sensitive baseline state.
- The brain's internal reward architecture undergoes a complete structural reset.
- Consequently, your mind reclaims the capacity to harvest deep, organic joy and *contentment* from the foundational realities of life. This fasting protocol delivers an absolute resurrection to your exhausted neurons.

The Neurobiology of Helper's High: The Corporate Bio-Shield

The execution of selfless service is far grander than a simplistic moral ideology; it is backed by an incredibly dense, documented neurobiological framework. When clinical researchers at Harvard University executed neuro-imaging structural scans of individuals who regularly commit their energy to anonymous, selfless service, they discovered an immediate activation of the brain's **Ventral**

Striatum. This is the exact cerebral region responsible for the processing of profound internal fulfillment and deep safety.

When you mobilize this dual cascade of oxytocin and serotonin via *Helper's High*, your physiology constructs an impenetrable biological shield against stress:

- It induces an instantaneous down-regulation of arterial blood pressure.
- It safely deactivates your hyperactive Sympathetic Nervous System, immediately mobilizing the Parasympathetic Nervous System (Rest and Digest mode).
- It optimizes your Heart Rate Variability (HRV), completely neutralizing the systemic risk of corporate burnout and chronic silent stress. Our ancient ancestors long ago coded this truth into the phrase *'Parhit saris dharam nahi bhai'*—proving that elevating the reality of another human being is the ultimate mechanism to unlock the neurochemical rebirth of your own brain.

The Gut-Brain Axis: The Secret Reservoir of 95% of Your Serotonin

When contemporary culture contemplates the hormone of sustainable contentment—serotonin—we instinctively assume its synthesis takes place exclusively within the neural networks of the brain. However, advanced discoveries within contemporary microbiology and neuro-gastroenterology have exposed a clinical reality that completely reconfigures our understanding of mental health: **95% of the human body's serotonin is synthesized not within the brain, but inside the tissues of our gastrointestinal tract (The Gut).** Clinically recognized as the **Gut-Brain Axis**, this biological highway connects your stomach and your skull via an unrelenting, real-time bi-directional superhighway called the **Vagus Nerve**.

Teeming within your digestive tract are trillions of microscopic organisms collectively known as the **Gut Microbiome**. When you operate under chronic corporate stress, logging 14-hour days before monitors while relying entirely on highly processed fast food, excessive synthetic sugars, and toxic levels of caffeine, you actively alter your internal ph balance, systematically executing the good bacteria of your microbiome.

- The exact second your internal gut ecosystem is compromised, your body's biological synthesis of serotonin collapses immediately.
- Consequently, the gut transmits an immediate emergency alert up the vagus nerve, forcing your brain into a state of severe clinical depression, unprovoked panic, and intense cognitive irritability.

Thousands of years ago, ancient Indian Ayurvedic sciences explicitly documented this exact biological reality, formulating the foundational maxim: *'Sarveshamapi rogaanaam nidaanam kupitaa malaah'*—establishing that the absolute root of every pathology, whether manifesting as a physical disease or an acute mental disorder, resides entirely within the health of the gut. When you feed your biology fresh, organic, whole foods, you nurture your microbiome. These microscopic organisms respond by producing a massive wave of pristine serotonin, transmitting it directly to your brain. Genuine contentment is not merely a philosophical concept; it is deeply rooted in the biological health of your stomach. When your gut is clean, balanced, and serene, your prefrontal cortex becomes naturally unhackable.

Real-Life Case Study: *The Chemical Awakening of 45-Year-Old Anand*

To map the absolute practical power of these neurochemical protocols into real-world dimensions, let us analyze the reality of 45-

year-old Anand (Assumed Name), who operated as a Senior Vice President at an elite, multi-national technology enterprise in Bengaluru. Anand possessed every single material trophy of modern success—a luxury vehicle fleet, a sprawling estate, and immense corporate authority. Yet, behind this external opulence, Anand's internal biology was entirely enslaved by a solitary, toxic chemical: artificial dopamine. He spent his existence running frantically after escalating corporate targets, the real-time volatility of financial markets, and the permanent incoming stream of critical enterprise emails. The direct biological consequence was severe: he succumbed to advanced clinical depression, intense digital anxiety, and total insomnia. The most premium pharmaceutical interventions and psychiatric evaluations across the globe failed to stabilize his fractured mood.

Desperate to escape this psychological decay, Anand committed to systematically applying the exact neuro-chemical parameters outlined within this text. He recognized that his internal dopamine loop had been completely weaponized against him, reducing his baseline serotonin and oxytocin reserves to absolute zero. He enforced two minor, non-negotiable modifications to his daily routine:

1. **The Morning Neuro-Reset:** He established an ironclad rule prohibiting the touch of any digital monitor for the first two hours of his day. Instead, he walked barefoot across untamed green spaces, dedicating fifteen minutes to **Vedic Chanting and Pranayama** (deep diaphragmatic breathwork). This targeted protocol immediately stabilized and elevated his brain's baseline **serotonin** levels.

2. **The Weekend Oxytocin Armor:** He committed to dedicating every Saturday evening to personally teaching mathematics and computing to orphaned children at a local community sanctuary (*Seva*).

Within a brief three-month window, Anand's internal cerebral chemistry underwent a complete transformation. The exact equilibrium that premium pharmacology failed to deliver was seamlessly established by his lifestyle modifications. The moment he sat with the orphaned children, sharing laughter and transferring knowledge, his neurobiology experienced such a monumental surge of **oxytocin** that his accumulated corporate stress and circulating cortisol were instantly neutralized. The morning breathwork and radical gratitude stabilized his emotional baseline. Today, Anand executes his corporate operations with greater strategic genius than ever before, but he no longer operates as a captive to his internal chemistry—he reigns as its absolute king. Anand's transformation stands as living proof that when you abandon the artificial dopamine loop and restore your D.O.S.E. protocol through organic, natural methodologies, your brain possesses the absolute power to heal itself.

CONCLUSION: Reign as the Sovereign King of Your Internal Chemistry

The exhaustive neuroscientific and ancient global data detailed across this eighth chapter establishes an unyielding biological truth: authentic, permanent, and unhackable happiness (*Santosha*) does not reside within a material object, a luxury asset, or a digital update. It belongs exclusively to the conscious, natural management of your internal neurochemical laboratory. Until you make a sovereign decision to halt your frantic pursuit of artificial digital dopamine and actively mobilize your organic reserves of oxytocin, serotonin, and endorphins, escaping the modern cage of chronic burnout remains a biological impossibility. Contentment is never an act of weakness or a compromise with failure; it is the absolute highest, most scientifically advanced operational state of the human brain.

A Personal Message from Hanika Deepchand

My dear readers, your magnificent brain is the most sacred, powerful, and miraculous laboratory in the entire known universe. Refuse to let it be poisoned by the digital garbage of corporate algorithms and the toxic cortisol of unrelenting stress. The exact moment you step out into nature to offer profound gratitude to this universe, the exact moment you extend your hand in absolute anonymity to elevate another human life without wanting anything in return, and the exact moment you sit in pristine internal immobility to anchor your consciousness—you are unlocking the secret code of contentment. You are activating a biological fortress that no digital technology can ever hack.

Claim your crown as the absolute king of your own internal laboratory. Awake to the majestic peace that belongs to you by birthright, because the absolute blueprint of your eternal joy is already written inside your biology—it is simply waiting for you to deliver its daily, natural D.O.S.E. Stand up, conquer your chemistry, and submerge your life in the light of unhackable joy.

LESSON 9

Failure to Happiness: The Art of Bouncing Back

Introduction: The Neurological Trauma of Defeat and the Reality of Resilience

It is an unyielding, absolute rule of human existence that no individual has ever walked the earth without tasting the bitter residue of failure or navigating an acute personal defeat. The catastrophic collapse of a high-stakes corporate campaign, the sting of an academic rejection, or the sudden dissolution of an enterprise represent situations that fundamentally destabilize the human spirit. Yet, contemporary society suffers from a severe psychological pathology: it has rigorously trained us to obsessively celebrate the illusion of superficial success, while offering absolutely zero preparation for the exact moment our physical bodies crash against the stone floor of reality.

The uncultivated mind views dropping into a state of profound depression and chronic self-condemnation following a defeat as an unalterable biological reflex. However, advanced empirical investigations within modern neuroscience definitively establish that maintaining absolute internal tranquility amidst failure, safeguarding your organic well-being, and returning to the operational field with double the strategic velocity is a highly structured, masterable discipline. This is clinically classified as 'The Art of Bouncing Back' or psychological resilience. Failure is never a definitive terminal point; it is a vital evolutionary input designed specifically to shock your cerebral architecture into a grander state of structural capacity.

The Neurobiological Reality of Failure: The Pain Coordinates of the Skull

When a human being experiences a significant professional defeat, the trauma is far deeper than a mere floating psychological thought. Through advanced neurological imaging scans, clinical science has proven that failure maps onto human biology as a literal, physical laceration.

- **The Matrix of Physical Pain vs. Abstract Loss:** Functional brain mapping (fMRI) demonstrates that when an individual experiences acute professional rejection, the **Anterior Cingulate Cortex**—the exact neural hub responsible for registering real physical injury—fires instantaneously. When a corporate enterprise dismisses your creative efforts, your brain does not register it as an intellectual disagreement; it processes the event as a direct physical strike to your survival.
- **The Amygdala Crisis Vector:** The exact micro-second a defeat manifests, the biological fire alarm inside your skull—the **Amygdala**—enters a state of hyper-arousal. It commands your adrenal glands to trigger an immediate, toxic inundation of systemic cortisol throughout your bloodstream. This chemical flooding completely blinds your rational faculties, generating deep-seated inadequacy and chronic clinical anxiety.

- **The Catastrophic Dopamine Crash:** Throughout the execution of any major life objective, the brain relies heavily on a steady baseline of dopamine to fuel its motivation pathways. The sudden collision with failure triggers an immediate, absolute drop in this chemical reserve, known as a **Dopamine Crash**. This sudden chemical deficit leaves the human system completely depleted and hollow from within. However, the sovereign observer who has mastered the art of bouncing back purposefully deploys their **Prefrontal Cortex** to immediately quiet this automated amygdala alarm, neutralizing the panic cycle before it can compromise their internal sovereignty.

Ancient Perspectives: Samatvam Yoga and the Alchemy of Neutrality

The exact structural resilience that contemporary neuroscience is mapping inside modern clinical facilities was completely established thousands of years ago across the battlegrounds of ancient India as the primary anchor of human psychological survival. In the second chapter of the *Srimad Bhagavad Gita*, when the warrior Arjuna was paralyzed by acute mental trauma, Lord Krishna delivered a monumental psychological code designed to convert the raw weight of failure into an absolute state of inner sovereign joy:

Yogasthah kuru karmani sangam tyaktva dhananjaya ।

Siddhy-asiddhyoh samo bhutva samatvam yoga uchyate ॥

Translation: (Bhagavad Gita – Chapter 2, Verse 48) *"Perform your duty with absolute steadfastness, O Arjuna, completely relinquishing your neurotic attachment to the outcome. Remain completely equanimous, balanced, and unchanged in both Siddhi (success) and Asiddhi (failure). This absolute internal neutrality, this divine equilibrium of the consciousness, is defined as Yoga (Samatvam)."*

The neuro-chemical mechanics embedded within this timeless verse reveal a profound cognitive blueprint:

1. **The Architecture of Success (Siddhi):** Refusing to surrender your awareness to the inflation of the ego when victory manifests, thereby preventing an unnatural dopamine spike that compromises your long-term cognitive judgment.
2. **The Architecture of Defeat (Asiddhi):** Refusing to descend into severe clinical depression when failure strikes, ensuring that a toxic inundation of cortisol is biologically blocked from destroying your executive faculties.

When you train your consciousness to interpret both polarities merely as neutral biological data strings or essential evolutionary lessons, your amygdala loses its power to hijack your physiology. Throughout ancient history, the legendary warriors and spiritual masters of India manifested this exact *Samatvam* code. They suffered repeated military collapses, lost empires, and navigated deep geographical exile, yet the structural integrity of their **Inner Citadel** remained completely unbroken. They transcended the dualities of victory and defeat, remaining immovably anchored within their core sovereign purpose.

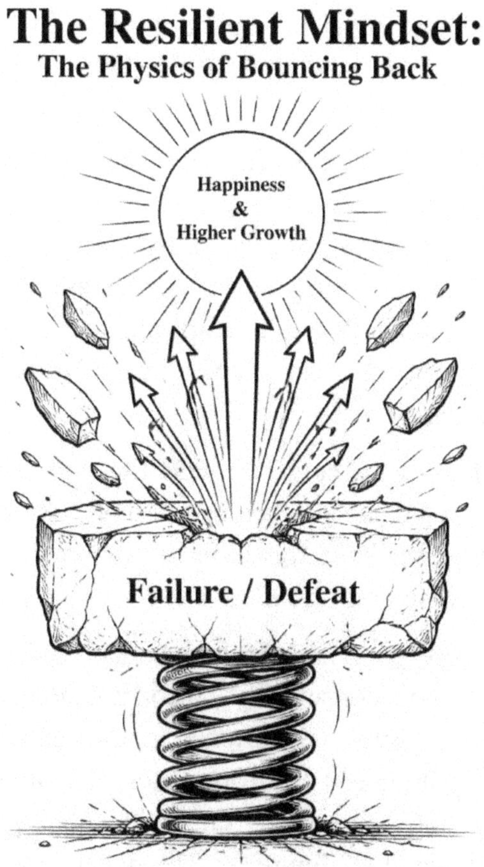

The Neuro-Mechanical Model of Resilience — How the intense pressure of professional defeat compresses our internal capabilities to trigger a grander velocity of growth and recovery.

The Science of Post-Traumatic Growth: Forging the Neural Steel

We must force our deep research to articulate an unyielding biological truth: failure is not a cultural inconvenience; it is a non-negotiable neurobiological necessity required to optimize the functional capacity of the human brain. For decades, traditional psychiatry remained heavily fixated on the pathological symptoms of Post-Traumatic Stress Disorder (PTSD). However, cutting-edge neuro-clinical networks are currently shifting their focus toward a magnificent biological phenomenon recognized as **Post-Traumatic Growth (PTG)**.

This breakthrough framework proves that when a human organism experiences a severe, life-altering psychological shock or material defeat, the rigid, pre-conditioned cognitive structures of their brain are completely shattered. Following this systematic deconstruction, the mechanisms of self-directed neuroplasticity ignite with immense velocity, forging entirely brand-new, robust neural connections across the cerebral cortex.

- Individuals who coast through life encountering effortless, uninterrupted success possess an executive brain architecture that has never been forced to test its structural boundaries; it remains inherently fragile.
- Conversely, the human being who has repeatedly crashed into failure and consciously reconstructed their awareness develops a Prefrontal Cortex that has been tempered like steel inside a furnace. Failure operates as a literal **neurological vaccine** for your mind, safely inoculating your biological systems against future existential crises, rendering you completely immune to environmental shock.

The Reframing Protocol: Transforming Defeat into Leverage

To insulate your neural networks from entering a downward spiral of depression the exact micro-second a failure strikes, you must systematically execute the three precise stages of the **Reframing Protocol**:

1. **Radical Cognitive Distancing:** Immediately command your internal dialogue to declare: *"I am not a failure; an objective execution I initiated has simply failed to deliver the anticipated metrics."* Your defeat is an isolated environmental

event; it is never your human identity. This simple, clinical separation instantly shields your baseline self-esteem from cortisol-driven decay.

2. **Scientific Data Extraction:** Completely refuse to descend into emotional sorrow or spend your priceless energy cursing your environment. Sit down with absolute stoic detachment, open your journal, and analyze the terrain like an objective researcher. Demand an answer to this question: *"What specific operational metric has this defeat exposed that an easy victory would have kept hidden from my awareness?"* Extracting raw data from your errors is the first real step of a strategic bounce back.

3. **The Activation of the Micro-Step:** Halt your brain from contemplating the massive, overwhelming weight of long-term consequences. Force your focus down to a hyper-localized horizon, giving your prefrontal cortex a highly simple, completely masterable task to execute over the next sixty minutes. The moment you complete this microscopic objective, your brain triggers a fresh, safe release of organic **dopamine** into your supressed receptors, instantly re-igniting your internal confidence.

The Labyrinth of Learned Helplessness and Neural Re-Conditioning

When a human being encounters repeated, consecutive failures across a compressed timeframe, their cerebral architecture is highly vulnerable to sliding into a hazardous psychological trap clinically defined as **Learned Helplessness**. According to neurobiological parameters, when continuous, exhaustive labor repeatedly returns a negative outcome, the Prefrontal Cortex mistakenly concludes that external environments are completely beyond its direct manipulation, internalizing a toxic belief: *"No matter what strategic adjustments I execute, my defeat is mathematically guaranteed."*

This dangerous state triggers immediate biological decay inside the skull:

- **The Collapse of Volition:** The brain completely halts the synthesis of vital neurochemicals required to generate willpower, motivation, and physical execution energy.
- **The Auto-Pilot Depressive Cascade:** The individual begins to experience a chronic state of isolated paralysis and systemic helplessness, even when an open path to victory reveals itself right before their eyes.

Dismantling this invisible trap requires the strict application of **Neuronal Re-Conditioning**. You must deliberately bypass the brain's defense networks by feeding it hyper-microscopic, completely certain goals for a continuous window of five to seven days. Every single time you achieve these minor, unchallenging targets, your brain receives a fresh wave of positive neurological feedback declaring: *"Winning is still a biological possibility within this system."* This targeted training protocol systematically erases the neural loops of learned helplessness, instantly liberating your internal resilience machinery.

The Chronicles of History: The Sacred Architecture of Strategic Retreat

Our deep research must expose a historical truth: for the greatest leaders and legendary tacticians of the ancient world, failure was never treated as an existential crisis; it was handled as a legitimate, functional variable within their overarching grand strategy. Ancient Indian military sciences utilized a highly sophisticated, profound term for this operational choice: **Strategic Retreat**.

When legendary sovereigns like Chhatrapati Shivaji महाराज or Maharana Pratap identified that the environmental forces stacked against them possessed an overwhelming material advantage, rendering a direct confrontation mathematically fatal, they purposefully abandoned the battlefield and withdrew deep into the sanctuary of the mountains and jungles. A superficial observer would instantly classify this movement as a definitive failure or an act of cowardice. Yet, history stands as an unyielding witness that it was nothing of the sort. It represented a highly calculated chronological window dedicated entirely to:

- Systematically restructuring, retraining, and reinforcing their combat forces.
- Executing a ruthless, deep evaluation of the predator's structural vulnerabilities.
- Constructing entirely brand-new, impregnable fortresses across superior terrain.

This ancient blueprint of a strategic retreat is your highest shield when navigating modern corporate burnout or a devastating personal defeat. The exact moment an enterprise collapses or a career path strikes a monumental wall, refuse to stay on that broken ground wasting your energy in self-blame. Execute a sovereign retreat. Step completely away from the digital rat race and the hyper-accelerated expectations of the crowd. Dedicate this quiet window of isolation to fortifying your internal fortress, allowing your neuroplastic circuits to carve fresh pathways, and sinking your consciousness back into absolute peace. Remember, even the apex predator of the jungle pulls its body back two paces before launching an earth-shattering leap. A strategic retreat does not weaken your execution; it equips you with the raw power of the universe before launching you back onto the field of destiny.

Real-Life Case Study: *The Rebirth of 38-Year-Old Vikram*

To study the absolute practical execution of these integrated ancient and modern protocols, let us analyze the lived reality of 38-year-old Vikram (Assumed Name), an intensely passionate tech entrepreneur operating out of Delhi. Vikram had committed his entire financial savings, along with a massive capital loan secured from elite banking institutions, to launch a disruptive startup within the hyper-competitive Educational Technology (Ed-Tech) sector. He logged exhausting hours day and night, completely anchoring his entire human self-worth onto the public success of this commercial enterprise. However, due to sudden, volatile macroeconomic shifts and a sequence of strategic miscalculations, Vikram's startup collapsed into absolute bankruptcy within twenty-four months. His enterprise closed its doors, his life's labor evaporated, and he was left buried beneath an immense mountain of financial debt.

This monumental defeat completely shattered Vikram's psychological foundation. He descended into a state of severe, clinical depression. His amygdala entered a state of permanent hijack, flooding his system with unmitigated anxiety. He experienced chronic insomnia, spending his nights locked in an agonizing loop of self-condemnation, viewing himself as an absolute, unmitigated loser. He internalized a distorted narrative that his life was effectively finished.

It was during this dark season of absolute desolation that Vikram initiated a deep study of this text, internalizing the mechanics of the neuroscientific **Reframing Protocol** and the Gita's code of **Samatvam**. He realized that he had committed the ultimate scientific error: he had allowed an external environmental event to define his internal human identity. He immediately halted his panic and deployed the protocols:

1. **The Separation of Identity:** He woke up every morning and explicitly instructed his neural networks: "My commercial startup has collapsed; I have not. My core capability as an elite software architect remains completely intact."

2. **Scientific Error Analysis:** He detached his emotions from the defeat, sitting with a pen and paper to trace every operational misstep that compromised his business. He chose to reframe

the entire bankruptcy as an incredibly expensive, premium business education.

3. **The Micro-Action Blueprint:** He completely abandoned the urge to immediately launch another massive venture, forcing his brain to focus exclusively on executing micro-consulting freelance assignments for small firms.

Within a brief six-month window of this disciplined execution, Vikram's internal cerebral chemistry achieved a state of perfect, harmonious equilibrium. His clinical depression vanished entirely. Emerging directly from the ash of that monumental bankruptcy, Vikram not only cleared his entire financial debt, but today he sits enthroned as the **Chief Technology Officer (CTO)** at one of the largest technology conglomerates in India. Vikram's transformation stands as a blazing warning to this world: when you refuse to let failure define your identity, and instead process it through the cosmic lens of *Samatvam*, there is zero power in any environmental defeat capable of hacking your internal joy.

CONCLUSION: Elevating the Fractured Spirit to the Horizon of Victory

The exhaustive neurological and timeless philosophical data detailed across this ninth chapter establishes an unyielding, crystalline truth: the path leading from the depth of failure to the absolute heights of permanent joy is not an accidental miracle; it represents the precise, practical application of a reconfigured cognitive perspective. Failure does not visit the human organism to weaken its structures; it arrives specifically to fortify the walls of your Inner Citadel. Until you weave the ancient equanimity of *Samatvam* with the modern science of cognitive reframing, you will remain buried beneath the debris of your circumstances. Mastering the art of bouncing back is the absolute validation of an unhackable human life.

A Personal Message from Hanika Deepchand

My dear readers, if you are currently standing at a crossroads in your life where you feel entirely defeated, broken, or consumed by the shadow of failure—know this with absolute, unbending certainty as you touch this physical page: no material defeat is grander than the infinite consciousness you carry within your being. Do not allow the limitless resilience and universe-given genius slumbering inside your neural pathways to be drowned in the tears of a temporary rejection or a financial loss.

Stand up. Brush the dust of that defeat off your clothes, close your physical eyes, and inhale a deep, magnificent breath of life. Success and failure are nothing more than passing waves undulating across the screen of existence; you are the immortal, completely unhackable warrior playing the game. Awake to your inner sovereignty. Master the art of bouncing back this very hour, and show this entire world that taming a quiet, awakened mind is a mathematical impossibility for any force in this universe. You are profoundly enough, you are entirely unbreakable, and you are destined for absolute victory.

PART 3

The Unhackable Protocols

LESSON 10

The Joy Protocol & Micro-Happiness

Introduction: The Delusion of Monumental Goals and the Erasure of the Present

Contemporary social programming has ruthlessly re-engineered the human cognitive apparatus to place extreme, highly unrealistic conditions on the experience of joy. The average individual operates under a toxic mental paradigm: they believe that they are only permitted to experience genuine fulfillment when they secure an elite corporate promotion, purchase an opulent residential estate, cross a massive numerical threshold in their bank statement, or embark on a luxurious international vacation. We have systematically surrendered our immediate happiness to the hypothetical realization of distant, monumental milestones.

However, the primary psychological cost of chasing these rare, outsized events is that our daily, 24-hour baseline existence begins to feel profoundly monotonous, uninspiring, and saturated with chronic friction. In anticipation of a singular, distant victory, we willingly sacrifice thousands of pristine, unrepeatable days to an internal state of quiet desperation. Both contemporary clinical neuroscience and ancient world philosophies completely dismantle this cognitive illusion.

Authentic, sustainable well-being does not reside within a future milestone; it is safely accessed exclusively by consciously savoring the tiny, 1-minute intervals of existence hidden within your ordinary day. Within the architecture of this text, this discipline is defined as 'Micro-Happiness'—the operational execution of 'The Joy Protocol.' This chapter serves as your practical manual to unleash an unrelenting cascade of internal peace right from the center of your hyper-busy, otherwise monotonous routine.

The Neurobiology of Micro-Happiness: Mobilizing the Micro-Dopamine Cascade

When a human organism successfully accomplishes a massive, long-term objective, the brain's internal reward network fires a massive, volatile explosion of the neurotransmitter **Dopamine**. However, clinical neurobiology proves that this massive chemical surge possesses a highly compressed half-life. Within an incredibly brief chronological window, the neural circuits adapt, forcing your emotional baseline to crash back down to its initial state of quiet dissatisfaction. In psychiatric science, this self-defeating loop is recognized as the **Hedonic Treadmill**—the biological law ensuring that no matter how much material wealth or status an individual accumulates, their baseline happiness remains completely stagnant.

Conversely, the deliberate practice of **Micro-Happiness** radically reconfigures the operational parameters of your cerebral architecture:

- **The Mechanism of Micro-Spikes:** The exact moment you halt your frantic routine for a solitary minute to observe the natural geometry of clouds, consciously internalize the exact warmth of your morning tea, or extend an authentic, unmanipulated smile to a peer, your brain executes a highly secure, pristine release of dopamine and serotonin. This is a **Neurochemical Micro-Spike**.

- **Systemic Neural Rewiring:** According to the unyielding laws of self-directed neuroplasticity, while these intervals span a mere sixty seconds, consistently acknowledging ten to twelve micro-spikes throughout your daily timeline systematically raises your baseline dopamine threshold.
- **The Immediate Cortisol Reset:** These deliberate intervals act as a manual override button for your nervous system, forcing your hyperactive **Amygdala** into a state of temporary suspension multiple times a day. This immediate pause abruptly drops systemic cortisol levels, signaling your biology that it is entirely safe to exit survival mode and enter a state of deep restoration.

Ancient Perspectives: The Upanishadic Paradox of 'Bhuma' vs. 'Alpa'

Thousands of years before contemporary research facilities mapped the mechanics of the hedonic treadmill, the ancient seers of India completely decoded this psychological trap within the sacred verses of the *Upanishads*. A foundational axiom delivered within the *Chandogya Upanishad* explicitly establishes: **"Yo vai bhuma tat sukham nalpe sukhamasti."** Superficially, untrained translators interpret this to mean that happiness exists only within immense physical scale, and cannot reside within small parameters. However, when we analyze this text with profound neuro-philosophical depth, a brilliant, transformative reality reveals itself.

Timeless wisdom does not define *Bhuma* as a massive material asset; **Bhuma represents the infinite, immeasurable depth locked within the immediate present moment.** Conversely, *Alpa* represents the hyper-narrowed, toxic state of chasing transient, finite, and external desires across a hypothetical future.

- The ancient sages explicitly warned that the exact second you sacrifice the sacred reality of the present moment to chase a future milestone, you become a captive of the *Alpa* matrix—an ecosystem of permanent internal scarcity and suffering.
- Conversely, when you bring the absolute entirety of your conscious awareness to savor a single minute of a simple sensory input—such as the texture of a breath of air or the warmth of a beverage—you break the illusion of linear time. Within that solitary minute, you experience *Bhuma*—the infinite expanse of cosmic consciousness.

Similarly, classical Buddhist psychologies anchored their entire framework onto **The Celebration of Impermanence (Anicca)** and pristine mindfulness. Life is not an industrialized race culminating at a specific commercial finish line; it is a dynamic, fluid river undulating through the current millisecond. Learning to extract absolute fulfillment from every singular drop of this river is the highest evolutionary and psychological truth.

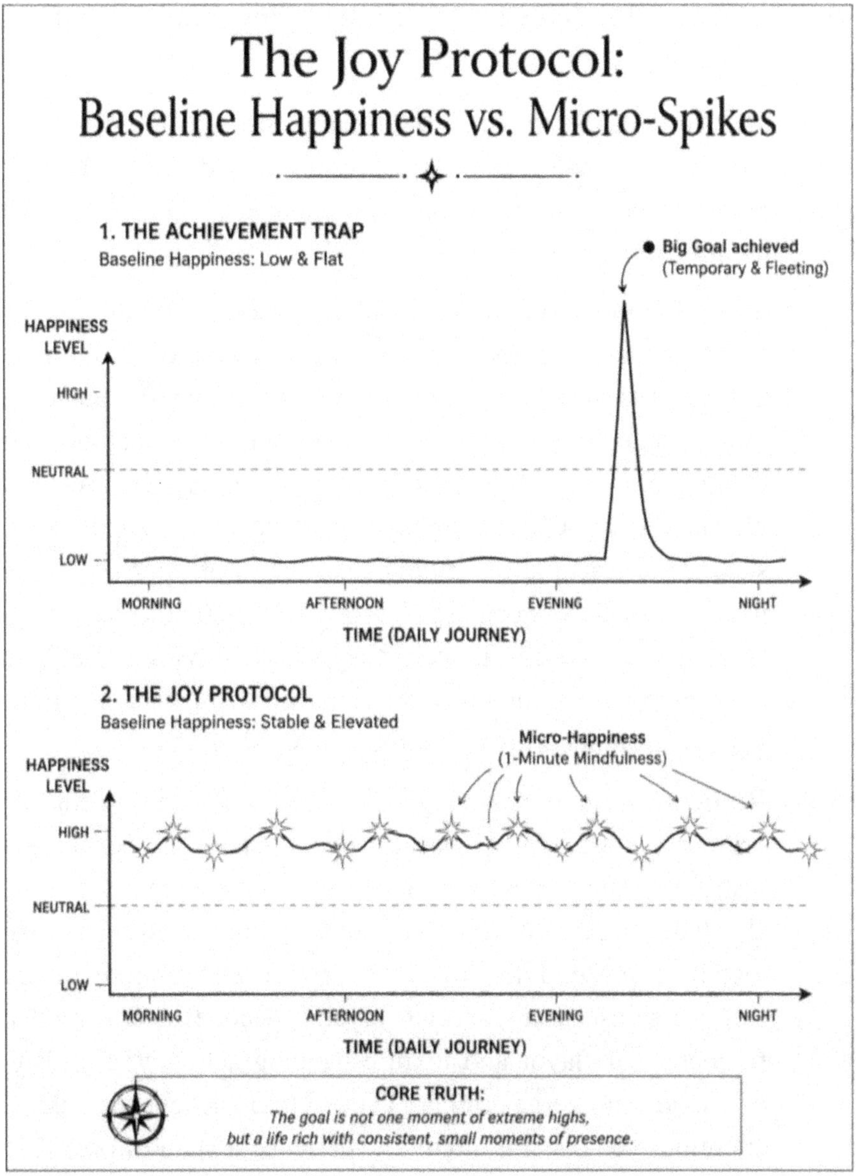

The Analytical Graph of the Joy Protocol — How micro-spikes of conscious mindfulness systematically elevate and stabilize the brain's internal emotional baseline compared to the volatile crash of monumental milestones.

The Joy Protocol: Three Precise Neuro-Cognitive Tools

To transform the discipline of micro-happiness into an unyielding, automated habit amidst the high-pressure landscape of your contemporary routine, you must systematically weaponize the following three precise tools:

1. **The 1-Minute Anchor:** Establish three non-negotiable check-points across your daily timeline (such as the exact moment before initiating workspace execution, the immediate center of your midday interval, and the exact second you conclude your evening commute). Completely place all digital devices out of physical sight. Close your eyes and dedicate exactly sixty seconds to tracking the biological friction of your breath, or looking out at the open sky. During this internal anchor, your brain is prohibited from executing a task, solving a problem, or tracking a corporate target. This protocol instantly pulls your prefrontal cortex out of the industrial rat race.

2. **Radical Sensory Savoring:** The next time you execute an ordinary, mundane physical action—such as consuming water, bathing, or eating a basic meal—you must force the absolute entirety of your five sensory apparatuses into that localized space. Internalize the precise temperature of the water against your dermal layers; decode every hidden frequency of flavor and texture dancing across your palate. When you submerge ordinary actions into this level of pristine attention, your neural circuits experience a state of profound biological fulfillment.

3. **The Micro-Gratitude Blueprint:** Completely cease waiting for monumental cosmic miracles to validate your happiness. Instead, train your cognitive networks to register the immense micro-assets of your immediate environment, offering a silent,

deep "thank you" for subtle details—such as securing transit exactly on schedule, or accessing a pristine glass of cold water during a high-temperature afternoon. This micro-gratitude immediately triggers a safe release of **serotonin** across your synapses, neutralizing acute anxiety in real-time.

Overthrowing the Attention Economy: Reclaiming Your Sovereign Joy

We must force our deep research to address the कड़वा (bitter) economic architecture that actively prevents contemporary humans from accessing these 1-minute intervals of micro-happiness. Our modern global marketplace operates completely as an industrialized **Attention Economy**. Elite technology conglomerates, dominant social platforms, and hyper-optimized advertising agencies spend billions of dollars annually for a singular, aggressive purpose—to execute a systematic theft of your raw human attention.

- The exact micro-second you encounter an unmonitored 1-minute interval of stillness (such as waiting for an elevator or standing in a café queue), the engineered corporate algorithms instantly trigger an internal state of neurochemical restlessness within your skull.
- You become biologically incapable of enduring sixty seconds of silence, causing you to reflexively pull your smartphone out of your pocket to scroll through a feed.

The absolute moment you surrender to that impulse, you are selling your priceless micro-happiness to optimize a tech corporation's commercial profit margin. The Joy Protocol delivers the exact weapon required to reclaim absolute sovereignty over your attention. The next time a brief interval of unstructured time reveals itself, completely refuse to touch the device. Stand in absolute, unhurried stillness. Gaze at the architecture surrounding your physical form, observe the facial profiles of human beings around you, or simply submerge your mind in the pristine rhythm of your heartbeat. Protecting your consciousness from being harvested by these corporate algorithms is the ultimate act of modern rebellion.

The Deception of 'Glance Value' and Subconscious Mind Hacking

Within contemporary neuro-marketing research, an incredibly deceptive behavioral weapon is deployed against human psychology, scientifically classified as **Glance Value**. This metric maps the exact cognitive reality that occurs when an individual checks their mobile monitor for a mere single second under the illusion of an innocent purpose—such as verifying the current time. The raw truth is that within that single second, your **Subconscious Mind** has already completely absorbed, processed, and internalized the hyper-vibrant color spectrums, the aggressive psychological positioning of advertisements, and the toxic red dots of unread notifications glowing on the display.

According to advanced cognitive neuroscience, this single-second glance functions as a literal injection of a **Micro-Stress Vector** deep into your neural tissue:

- While your rational mind concludes that you merely looked at a clock, your internal biology responds by executing a micro-secretion of systemic cortisol into your bloodstream.
- This chronic accumulation of micro-stress quietly erodes your entire internal peace throughout the day, rendering you biochemically incapable of accessing or processing the frequencies of micro-happiness.

The Joy Protocol systematically severs this subconscious hacking trap. The exact moment you make a sovereign choice to track chronological time via a mechanical wall clock or a traditional wristwatch—completely bypassing the smartphone display—you insulate your subconscious mind from unwanted corporate data collection. This minor modification preserves your cognitive real estate, keeping your neural pathways clean, focused, and entirely unburdened by digital garbage.

The Law of Neuronal Satiation: Restoring Neurological Fulfillment

When you systematically activate the protocols of micro-happiness—specifically the discipline of Radical Sensory Savoring—you trigger a magnificent biological phenomenon within your skull known as **Neuronal Satiation**. Under normal modern parameters, when an individual consumes nutrients while simultaneously engaging with a digital monitor, the brain's sensory gating mechanisms are completely compromised; the neural circuits are blocked from processing the complex biochemical frequencies of the flavor profile. Consequently, while your physical stomach is filled with calories, your neurobiological reward system remains completely starved. This chemical starvation births a state of chronic psychological restlessness, forcing the individual into an ongoing state of hyper-consumption.

Conversely, the moment you bring the absolute totality of your attention to a localized action for a brief minute:

- Your firing neurons become completely saturated and satisfied by the pure biochemical feedback of that specific experience (such as the raw taste of nutrients or the cooling touch of a breeze).
- The prefrontal cortex transmits an immediate, definitive biological signal to your nervous system declaring: *"The organism has received exactly what it required; I am entirely content."*

This profound state of neurological fulfillment completely eradicates **Hoarding Behavior**—the chronic behavioral dependency to constantly buy, scroll, or consume material items to fill an inner void. The individual who masters the mechanics of neuronal satiation reclaims the status of a king while utilizing minimal resources. Their consciousness resides in a permanent sanctuary of deep tranquility and unhackable joy, because their emotional baseline has been entirely untethered from external commercial numbers and industrial gadgets.

Real-Life Case Study: *The Behavioral Metamorphosis of 29-Year-Old Kritika*

To observe the clinical execution of this neurochemical protocol within real-world boundaries, let us analyze the lived reality of 25-year-old Kritika (Assumed Name), who operated as a Data Analyst within an elite corporate consultancy in Mumbai. Her entire daily existence was consumed by sitting before a dark monitor, tracking massive excel datasets and numerical indices for ten hours a day. Kritika had deeply internalized a toxic belief that her life was entirely monotonous, exhausting, and devoid of authentic value. She lived in a permanent state of high irritability, operating under a rigid psychological contract that she would only permit herself to experience true happiness two years into the future—the specific milestone when her salary metrics would increase, allowing her to purchase an international vacation to Europe. By anchoring her well-being to this distant goal, she was treating her immediate days as a prison sentence.

The chronic friction brought Kritika to the absolute precipice of clinical workspace burnout; the mere thought of entering her office triggered acute waves of panic. Desperate for a remedy, she committed to deploying the protocols of **The Joy Protocol** and **Micro-Happiness** outlined within this text. She refused to initiate massive, disruptive lifestyle alterations; instead, she engineered three hyper-microscopic, 1-minute interventions directly into her dense corporate routine:

1. **The Witness Architecture of Tea:** During her brief evening interval at the office, she left her mobile device completely stationary on her executive desk. She spent five minutes holding the heated ceramic cup, internalizing its thermal signature against her palms, decoding the aroma frequencies, and consuming each sip without a single racing thought.
2. **The 60-Second Desk Reset:** After every three-hour block of dense data analysis, she purposefully turned her eyes away from the monitor, reinforced her spinal alignment, and dedicated exactly sixty seconds to tracking the rise and fall of her diaphragm.
3. **The Transit Symphony Protocol:** While navigating the high-stress environment of local mass transit trains, instead of checking social media feeds, she closed her eyes and listened to a singular, tranquil acoustic instrumental track, fully internalizing the sensation of the wind passing through the carriage window.

Within four weeks of this disciplined execution, an incredible, revolutionary metamorphosis manifested, completely astonishing her corporate peers. The workspace environment was entirely unchanged, the data monitors were identical, and the institutional pressure remained constant—yet Kritika had undergone a complete internal rebirth. Day after day, these micro-intervals had accumulated to trigger such a massive, sustained elevation of **serotonin and endorphins** across her neural networks that her chronic irritability and clinical burnout vanished entirely. She was no longer living as a captive to a hypothetical future vacation in Europe; she had reclaimed her status as the absolute sovereign ruler of the infinite joy hidden inside her ordinary, unedited days. Kritika's transformation stands as a blazing warning to this world: the moment you abandon the illusion of distant monumental goals and embrace the architecture of micro-happiness, your ordinary routine transitions into a magnificent celebration.

CONCLUSION: Gaze Inside the Micro-Second to Discover the Cosmos

The exhaustive neurobiological and deep philosophical investigation detailed across this tenth chapter establishes an unyielding, crystalline truth: 'The Joy Protocol' is not an external luxury or an accidental circumstance; it represents the precise, practical application of a highly trained attention span. Cease halting your life in anticipation of monumental future milestones, for sacrificing the sacred asset of your immediate day to a psychological illusion is the absolute definition of ignorance. When you train your consciousness to extract 1-minute bursts of micro-happiness from the texture of your ordinary routine, your brain becomes completely fortified, rendering your tranquility entirely unhackable by corporate stress or digital algorithms. Happiness is never a distant geographic destination; it is the sovereign discipline of taking every single step with absolute, mindful joy.

A Personal Message from Hanika Deepchand

My dear readers, this ordinary daily routine that you frequently label as monotonous or boring is, in absolute reality, a magnificent, priceless masterwork delivered to you by the universe. Within every single micro-interval of this existence—hidden deep inside the warmth of a tea cup, the innocent laughter of a child, and the immediate movement of your current breath—the entire cosmos is dancing in its absolute, unbridled glory. Refuse to let the false mirage of a future monumental goal burn the sacred asset of your immediate day into the ash of anxiety.

Halt the digital noise this very hour. Close your physical eyes, and submerge your awareness in the magical tranquility of the present moment. The exact second you claim sovereignty over a single minute of micro-happiness, there is zero power in any corporate algorithm or external stressor capable of hacking your eternal joy. Stand up. Transform your ordinary days into an absolute celebration, because within the boundaries of this immediate micro-second, you are already entirely complete, infinitely wealthy, and profoundly enough.

LESSON 11

The Digital Borderline

Introduction: Unseen Servitude and the Architecture of Boundaries

The contemporary human being exists in an era where geographic parameters and physical borders are guarded with absolute military precision, while the vital psychological and personal borders of their individual life have completely collapsed. Technology and the modern smartphone have successfully executed a deep penetration into the most sacred, private chambers of human existence—spaces that historically remained under the absolute sovereignty of the individual mind. When a corporate professional lies paralyzed in their bed at 11:00 PM manually processing enterprise emails, or when a young individual sacrifices their vital sleep to scroll through algorithmic social feeds until 3:00 AM, they are navigating an unmonitored state of digital servitude.

We initially adopted these digital interfaces to optimize our baseline operational convenience; today, however, these technologies have systematically commodified and captured our raw human attention, our foundational willpower, and our finite chronological time. To survive this ongoing cognitive assault, human consciousness demands the immediate enforcement of a non-negotiable, mathematically explicit **'Digital Borderline.'** This psychological boundary does not command you to develop a primitive hatred for technology; rather, it provides the precise blueprint required to reclaim your status as its absolute master. Until you build an impenetrable, structural wall between your daily screen time and your internal awareness, no premium clinical therapy or academic knowledge can liberate your biology from the loops of chronic corporate burnout and systemic digital anxiety.

Dopamine Fasting: The Neuro-Clinical Reality of Receptors Resets

The primary, highly revolutionary weapon deployed to secure this digital borderline is the clinical execution of **Dopamine Fasting**. As systematically mapped across the foundational chapters of this text, the unrelenting influx of software notifications, social media validations, and engineered infinity-scrolling architectures maintains the human brain in a state of permanent neurochemical over-saturation. When human cerebral tissue is subjected to this chronic state of hyper-stimulation, your delicate dopamine receptors automatically execute a defensive shutdown. Within neurobiology, this is classified as receptor down-regulation, leaving the individual feeling perpetually depleted, cognitively fractured, and intensely irritable.

Dopamine fasting is completely distinct from superficial cultural trends or abstract philosophical concepts; it represents a precise biological protocol engineered to manually reset your internal neural pathways:

- **The Mechanism of Receptor Up-regulation:** The exact moment you consciously restrict the influx of synthetic neurochemical triggers—completely severing interaction with mobile screens, algorithmic networks, and hyper-stimulating digital platforms for a dedicated window—your desensitized dopamine receptors initiate a process of **Up-regulation**. They systematically return to their natural, highly sensitive baseline capacity.

- **The Resurrection of Volition:** Throughout this structured fasting window, your over-exhausted **Prefrontal Cortex** is finally granted the biological environment required to exit survival operations and enter total restoration. Resetting your internal reward architecture triggers an immediate rebirth of deep concentration, ironclad self-regulation, and authentic human willpower. Your neurobiology reclaims the organic capacity to harvest profound satisfaction from foundational, real-world stimuli—such as contemplating natural ecosystems, interacting with long-form physical texts, or submerging your mind in absolute silence.

Screen-Free Zones: Constructing the Primal Fortresses of Quietude

The secondary, highly practical phase of enforcing your digital borderline requires the physical construction of non-negotiable **'Screen-Free Zones'** across your domestic environment and daily timeline. This parameter dictates that specific geographic vectors within your immediate environment must remain entirely insulated from the presence of any digital monitor, smartphone, laptop, or portable computing device.

Advanced neuropsychology proves that the human subconscious mind is continuously, deeply conditioned by the spatial parameters of its immediate physical architecture. If your mobile device rests directly adjacent to your pillow at night, your **Amygdala** remains biologically incapable of entering a state of absolute, restorative suppression during sleep cycles. The primitive survival centers of your brain remain chronically hyper-vigilant, fully aware that a high-velocity neurochemical trigger rests a mere hand's breadth away from your body.

By systematically enforcing the following three primary Screen-Free Zones, you infuse your neural networks with an unyielding shield of biological protection:

1. **The Bedroom Sanctuary:** Enforce an ironclad boundary prohibiting the entry of any mobile device into your sleeping quarters exactly sixty minutes before initiating rest and for the first sixty seconds following morning waking. Your bed must be preserved as a sacred space dedicated exclusively to physiological recovery and deep sleep, never as an active laboratory for algorithmic consumption.
2. **The Dining Table Protocol:** During the consumption of nutrients, every single device belonging to the domestic unit must be physically removed from the dining architecture and placed inside an entirely separate room. Force your focus to submerge completely into the chemistry of your food and the real-world frequencies of family dialogue.
3. **The Deep Work Pause:** When executing highly critical strategic objectives or deep creative assignments, your personal mobile device must be configured to an absolute 'Do Not Disturb' state and physically locked within an opaque executive desk drawer. Completely removing the screen from your immediate visual field instantly accelerates your deep focus capacity by an order of magnitude.

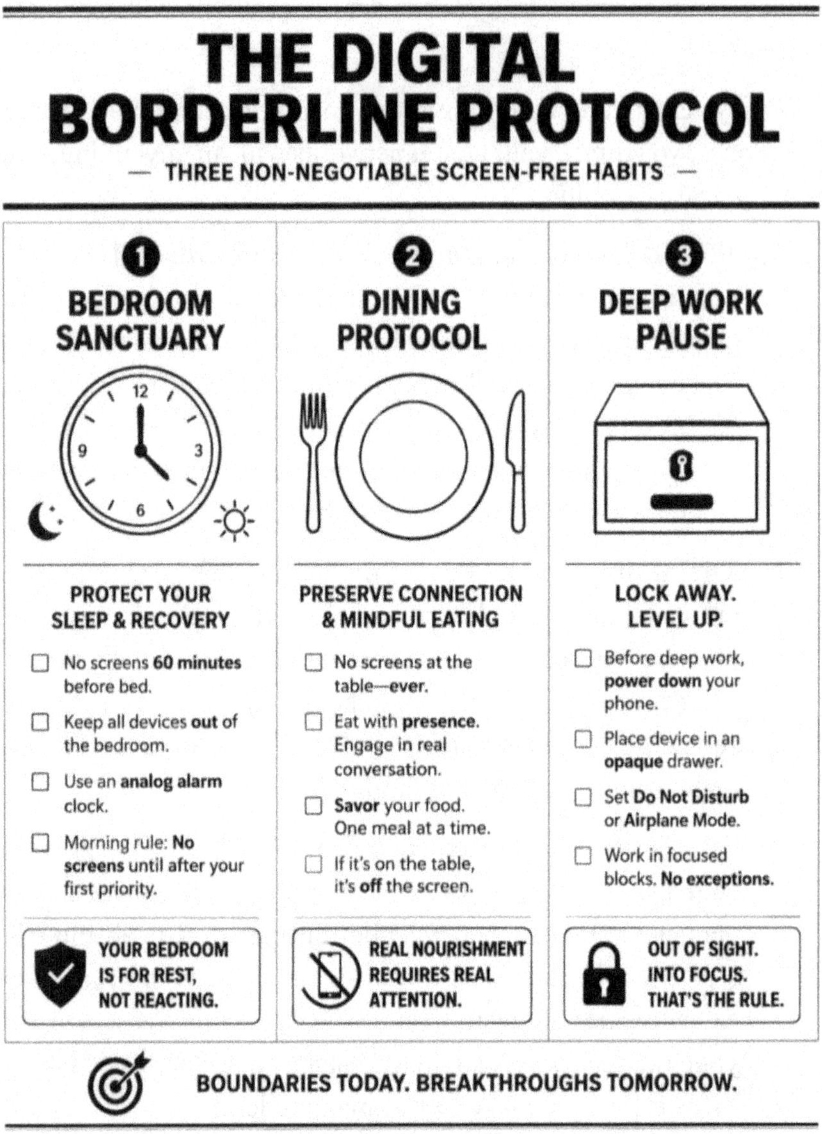

The Operational Matrix of the Digital Borderline — How the systematic enforcement of spatial screen-free zones and dopamine fasting shields human cerebral networks from external algorithmic manipulation.

The Digital Fasting Blueprint: A Step-by-Step Chronological Guide

To ensure contemporary corporate professionals and hyper-connected youth possess more than abstract theory, we must deliver a rigorous, highly structured execution matrix. Below is the non-negotiable, step-by-step **Digital Fasting Blueprint** engineered for immediate lifestyle integration:

- **Phase 1: The Daily 24-Minute Reset:** Immediately following the conclusion of your primary professional workspace execution, completely deactivate your mobile device for exactly twenty-four consecutive minutes. Dedicate this brief chronological window exclusively to silent introspection, physical decompression stretching, or observing the unedited environment outside your window. This targeted intervention down-regulates your Sympathetic Nervous System, immediately mobilizing your Parasympathetic architecture to halt the accumulation of silent stress.
- **Phase 2: The Weekend 12-Hour Absolute Fast:** Dedicate one specific day each week (optimally your Sunday interval) to executing a continuous twelve-hour digital fast, completely untethering your biology from internet matrices between 9:00 AM and 9:00 PM. Explicitly notify your professional and social networks beforehand that your digital avatar will remain entirely offline, and you can only be reached via a legacy basic analog device for legitimate life-or-death emergencies. Re-allocate this chronological window to navigating natural ecosystems, engaging in intense physical sport, or treading across long-abandoned creative hobbies.
- **Phase 3: The Quarterly 48-Hour Sovereign Retreat:** Once every ninety days, completely sever all interactions with digital communication matrices for an entire, uninterrupted forty-eight-hour weekend block. This clinical protocol allows

for deep synaptic pruning across your neural connections, systematically eradicating deep-seated chronic burnout and neurological fatigue at their biological roots.

The Pathology of Attention Leakage: The Chemical Warfare of Notifications

To maximize the academic density of our deep research, we must explore a micro-layered cognitive pathology clinically identified as **Attention Leakage**. Consider a scenario where you are sitting at your workspace desk completely focused on synthesizing a high-value data report. Suddenly, your mobile display illuminates due to an incoming social network notification or chat group update. Even if you manifest the structural willpower to refuse to physically pick up the device, a devastating chemical assault has already been executed inside your skull.

The exact millisecond that screen flashes its artificial luminescence:

- Your Prefrontal Cortex is involuntarily disengaged from the complex neural architecture of the task you were executing.
- Your subconscious networks immediately begin expending vital energy tracking an unverified narrative, demanding: *"What specific information is locked behind that glowing alert?"* In cognitive psychology, this fracture is recognized as **Cognitive Re-orientation**.
- Clinical empirical metrics prove that following a single second of this visual distraction, the human brain requires an average of **23 minutes and 15 seconds** of continuous cognitive friction simply to return to the exact same depth of focus it possessed before the screen flashed.

When this attention leakage is repeated dozens of times throughout a standard workspace day, your cognitive energy experiencing massive systemic bleeding, reducing your operational efficiency by fifty percent. The architecture of the Digital Borderline dictates that placing your device on a silent configuration is completely insufficient; it must remain **entirely removed from your immediate visual spectrum** (*Out of Sight, Out of Mind*). By systematically hiding the screen, you halt the pathology of attention leakage, completely securing your brain's vital energy for deep execution.

The Myth of Digital Nomadism: Reclaiming the Sanctity of Isolation

Our deep research must ruthlessly expose a massive cultural illusion that has completely colonized the psychology of the contemporary generation—the hyper-glorified mirage of **Digital Nomadism**, or the transactional narrative celebrating the freedom to execute corporate labor from any geographic vector on the planet. Contemporary culture dictates that responding to enterprise demands while sitting amidst mountain landscapes or editing media feeds inside coastal cafes constitutes absolute freedom. However, neurobiology proves that when you completely erase the structural borders separating your professional labor from your private existence, you have not achieved liberty; you have simply built the ultimate mental cage.

When you journey into a natural ecosystem under the guise of a vacation, yet continue to process corporate communications on your laptop, your **Amygdala** is biologically blocked from entering its evolutionary 'rest-and-recovery' configuration. The therapeutic, restorative frequencies of nature are completely blocked from healing your neural networks because your raw human attention remains tightly bound inside the prison of the digital cursor.

The Digital Borderline teaches an uncompromising truth: **your execution window belongs exclusively to execution, and your restoration window belongs entirely to absolute restoration.**

Constructing these rigid, structural boundaries is never an act of personal restriction; it is the absolute foundation of your psychological liberty and deep internal peace. By fiercely guarding your boundaries, you completely defeat a multi-billion-dollar corporate algorithm engineered to keep you locked as a permanent consumer 24 hours a day.

Real-Life Case Study: *The Liberation of 34-Year-Old Rahul*

To study the practical execution of this digital border protocol within real-world parameters, let us evaluate the reality of 34-year-old Rahul (Assumed Name), who operated as a Senior Creative Head at an elite ad agency in Mumbai. His professional landscape was saturated with extreme, high-velocity pressure, and he existed as an individual who possessed absolute zero structural boundaries. He initiated his daily existence by checking enterprise chat logs while still immobilized in his morning bed, remained chained to monitors throughout the afternoon, and routinely processed client communications at 2:00 AM. Rahul operated under a delusion that remaining permanently accessible was the sole driver of his professional acceleration.

The direct biological consequence of this unmonitored lifestyle was catastrophic. Within a brief three-year window, Rahul's neurochemical equilibrium fractured completely. He fell victim to severe, chronic insomnia, intense clinical irritability, and generalized anxiety disorders. His creative output decayed so severely that his campaign designs were repeatedly rejected by the enterprise board. While his physical frame occupied a seat at the corporate desk, his cognitive faculties were entirely paralyzed by profound neurological fatigue. His clinical physicians delivered an ultimatum: he was navigating the terminal stage of **Chronic Burnout Syndrome**, an executive boundary from which recovery is immensely difficult.

At the absolute lowest point of his life, Rahul committed to deploying the **Digital Borderline** protocols outlined within this text as a form of non-negotiable mental discipline. To reclaim his consciousness, he constructed three rigid, structural walls across his lifestyle:

1. **The 7:00 PM Lakshmi Rekha:** He dispatched an explicit directive to his creative team and enterprise clients declaring that at exactly 7:00 PM, his professional laptop and corporate devices would shut down completely, and he would remain entirely unreachable unless an absolute life-or-death emergency manifested.
2. **The Bedroom Sanctuary Implementation:** He completely banned the physical entry of any digital monitor into his sleeping quarters, replacing his morning screen scrolling with an uninterrupted hour dedicated exclusively to pranayama breathwork and long-form journaling.
3. **The Sunday Dopamine Fast:** He enforced an ironclad twelve-hour digital fast every single Sunday, completely separating his biology from the internet matrix between 9:00 AM and 9:00 PM.

The initial fourteen days of this transition were an absolute psychological battlefield for Rahul. His brain continuously screamed for its familiar chemical injection of notification dopamine, and he was violently attacked by waves of digital anxiety and intense FOMO. Yet, Rahul stood as an immovable fortress. According to the mechanics of self-directed neuroplasticity, at the 21-day threshold, his brain accepted the structural reality of this new stillness.

Within two months of this disciplined execution, Rahul's entire life path was completely rewritten. His chronic insomnia vanished entirely, allowing him to experience the deep, restorative sleep of a child. Grander still, his executive focus and innovative creative faculties returned with such monumental velocity that his next marketing campaign secured an elite international award for his enterprise. Rahul's transformation stands as a blazing proof to this world: the moment you draw a strict digital borderline against the encroachment of technology, you cease existing as an algorithmic slave; you claim your sovereign crown as the true king of your own consciousness.

CONCLUSION: Enforce Your Boundaries, Reclaim Your Absolute Freedom

The deeply practical, eye-opening neuroscientific evaluation detailed across this eleventh chapter establishes an unyielding truth: the 'Digital Borderline' is not a superficial technological choice; it represents the solitary scientific bio-shield required to preserve your psychological sanity in an hyper-accelerated era. Technology is not inherently evil, but the exact moment its structural borders encroach upon your sleeping sanctuary, your family dining experience, and the deep layers of your soul, it systematically extracts your natural happiness. Until you deliberately integrate these rigid protocols of dopamine fasting and spatial screen-free zones into your physical lifestyle, you will remain a helpless consumer dancing to the rhythm of a corporate algorithm. Drawing your border is the ultimate act of modern psychological liberation.

A Personal Message from Hanika Deepchand

My dear readers, your magnificent, priceless life and your internal consciousness belong entirely and exclusively to you—never to a corporate digital screen, an application interface, or a social network algorithm. As you read these words on this page today, draw an unyielding, absolute 'Digital Borderline' around your existence. Cultivate the sovereign courage to close your professional device the moment your work concludes, liberate your bedroom from the toxicity of digital garbage, and step out of the illusion of this artificial blue light.

While the external world screams frantically to harvest your attention for its profit margins, stand tall within your self-respect and declare: *"Stop! This chronological time belongs to me, this tranquility is my birthright, and there is zero external technology permitted to cross this border."* Cease surrendering your awareness to your notifications. Stand up. Reconfigure these boundaries as your highest source of strength, and show this entire digitized world that your mind sits enthroned upon the highest peaks of absolute freedom, entirely unhackable, and permanently at peace. Within your boundaries, you are limitless, you are completely sovereign, and you are profoundly enough.

LESSON 12
The Daily Reset: 5-Minute Brain Rituals

Introduction: The Biological Battery and the Urgent Need for a Manual Reboot

The contemporary human being exhibits a highly efficient behavioral pattern when managing material technology: the exact moment their laptop, smartphone, or peripheral device drops below a critical battery threshold, they immediately attach it to an industrialized electrical source. They comprehend with absolute clarity that failure to execute this simple intervention will result in the immediate shutdown of the apparatus. Yet, consider the supreme neuro-biological irony: this exact individual applies absolute zero preventative maintenance to the magnificent, priceless biological engine nestled directly inside their skull—the human brain. From the precise second of morning waking until they collapse back into bed at night, they subject their neural tissue to a relentless, high-voltage current of incoming data strings, urgent enterprise updates, and unmonitored digital notification loops.

The direct physiological consequence of this continuous overload is that by mid-afternoon, the brain's internal vital energy drops to absolute depletion. The organism falls captive to a severe, clinical state of Cognitive Fatigue—a literal mental paralysis where deep-work capacity fractures and memory recall stalls entirely.

The average corporate professional erroneously assumes that the solitary mechanism to recover from this exhaustion is to log extended sleep hours over weekends or escape to a distant geographic vacation. However, empirical neurological science explicitly shatters this paradigm. Just as you manually command a lagging desktop operating system to execute a definitive 'reboot,' you possess the absolute biological capability to completely reset your cerebral architecture in multiple intervals throughout the day—requiring a mere five minutes of your chronological time. Within this text, this targeted intervention is recognized as 'The Daily Reset.' This mental ritual is completely removed from abstract or superficial concepts; it constitutes a highly structured, clinical neuro-biological protocol engineered to re-oxygenate your neurons and systematically deactivate your hyperactive amygdala alarm.

The Neurobiology of the Daily Reset: Activating the Vagus Nerve Superhighway

To explicitly decode the near-miraculous transformation triggered across a brief 300-second window, we must evaluate a primary neural highway hidden within our autonomic nervous system, clinically classified as the **Vagus Nerve**. Originating directly within the intricate structures of the brainstem, the vagus nerve extends as the longest, most biologically influential cranial nerve across the human organism, directly interfacing with the heart, the pulmonary system, and the entire gastrointestinal tract. It serves as the primary master switch for our **Parasympathetic Nervous System** (the baseline rest-and-digest matrix).

When you operate under high-velocity workspace strain or chronic digital anxiety:

- Your Sympathetic Nervous System is kept in a permanent state of hyper-arousal, forcing an elevated resting heart rate and commanding a continuous secretion of systemic cortisol into your vascular channels.
- The exact micro-second you initiate a structured, 5-minute mental ritual (such as executing targeted, rhythmic diaphragmatic breathing patterns), you transmit an immediate, high-velocity electrical impulse down the vagus nerve superhighway.
- Upon registering this signal, the vagus nerve forces your cerebral networks to issue an immediate biological counter-mandate: slowing cardiopulmonary acceleration, safely down-regulating arterial blood pressure, and completely blocking the synthesis of cortisol. Within a brief 300 seconds, your entire biology exits survival parameters, anchoring itself in a state of absolute psychological safety. Through the mechanics of self-directed neuroplasticity, executing these brief manual reboots immediately doubles your cognitive efficiency and analytical clarity for the subsequent execution cycle.

The 5-Minute Brain Rituals: Three Unbreakable Protocols

This framework delivers three highly precise, non-negotiable mental rituals requiring a mere five minutes of your daily allocation, yet generating a transformative upgrade across your cognitive output:

1. The Morning Neuro-Priming Ritual

The exact moment you awaken, completely refuse to let the artificial blue light of a smartphone screen hijack your subconscious mind. Instead, reinforce your spinal alignment, sit upright in your bed, and execute the following:

- **The First 2 Minutes (Box Breathing):** Initiate a strict sequence of 'Box Breathing'—inhale deeply for exactly 4 seconds, hold the breath inside (*Kumbhaka*) for 4 seconds, exhale entirely over 4 seconds, and remain empty for 4 seconds. This targeted respiratory friction forces an immediate flood of highly oxygenated blood directly into the prefrontal cortex, instantly vaporizing morning cognitive sluggishness.

- **The Next 2 Minutes (Strategic Visualization):** Maintain absolute optical closure and deliberately pre-program your neural pathways by visualizing your day's top three Most Important Tasks (MITs), seeing yourself executing them with pristine concentration, absolute emotional stability, and strategic success.
- **The Final 1 Minute (Cosmic Gratitude):** Internally express a deep, unadulterated state of gratitude to the universe for the gift of life and the biological continuity of your breath. This 5-minute priming sequence safely inoculates your entire cerebral architecture against the encroachment of chronic silent stress throughout the day.

2. The Midday Amygdala Pause Ritual

The exact second a mid-afternoon cognitive wall manifests—typically between 2:00 PM and 3:00 PM—and your focus begins to scatter, completely deactivate your laptop screen, step away from digital monitors, and sit completely still in your chair:

- **The First 3 Minutes (The Physiological Sigh):** Execute the clinically proven **Physiological Sigh** protocol popularized by Stanford University laboratories—inhale deeply through your nasal passages twice consecutively (one long, deep inhalation instantly followed by a secondary, sharp micro-inhalation), then completely open your mouth to slow-release the entire breath. Neurobiology establishes that executing this specific sequence merely three times consecutively causes your collapsed pulmonary alveoli to immediately reinflate, dropping carbon dioxide concentrations in your bloodstream and dropping systemic stress by ninety percent in real-time.

- **The Final 2 Minutes (Thermal Palming Therapy):** Rub your physical palms together with high velocity until you generate significant friction-based biological heat. Immediately cup your warmed hands directly over your closed optical framework (**Palming**). This state of absolute pitch darkness combined with localized biological heat delivers profound neuro-muscular relaxation to your over-exhausted **Optic Nerve**, instantly dispersing mental fog.

3. The Night Cortisol Dump Ritual

Exactly fifteen minutes before preparing to initiate sleep cycles, completely remove all mobile devices from your sleeping sanctuary, sit at a cleared desk, and open a raw physical journal with an analog pen:

- **The Full 5 Minutes (The Brain Dump):** Begin aggressively transcribing every solitary thought, pending schedule, professional anxiety, unfinished corporate directive, and unstructured fear circulating across your awareness onto the paper without a single edit or self-correction. This clinical discipline is recognized as a **Brain Dump** or *Cortisol Deactivation.*
- The exact second you transmute these abstract, racing thoughts out of your skull and capture them into a tangible physical medium, your hyperactive **Amygdala** receives a structural signal proving that it is no longer biologically responsible for memorizing or tracking these internal threats. Consequently, systemic cortisol levels drop off a cliff, paving an unobstructed path for the immediate synthesis of **Melatonin** (the sleep hormone). This simple visual evacuation insulates your nervous system from the 'Tired but Wired'

matrix, anchoring your biology into the deep, restorative sleep of a child.

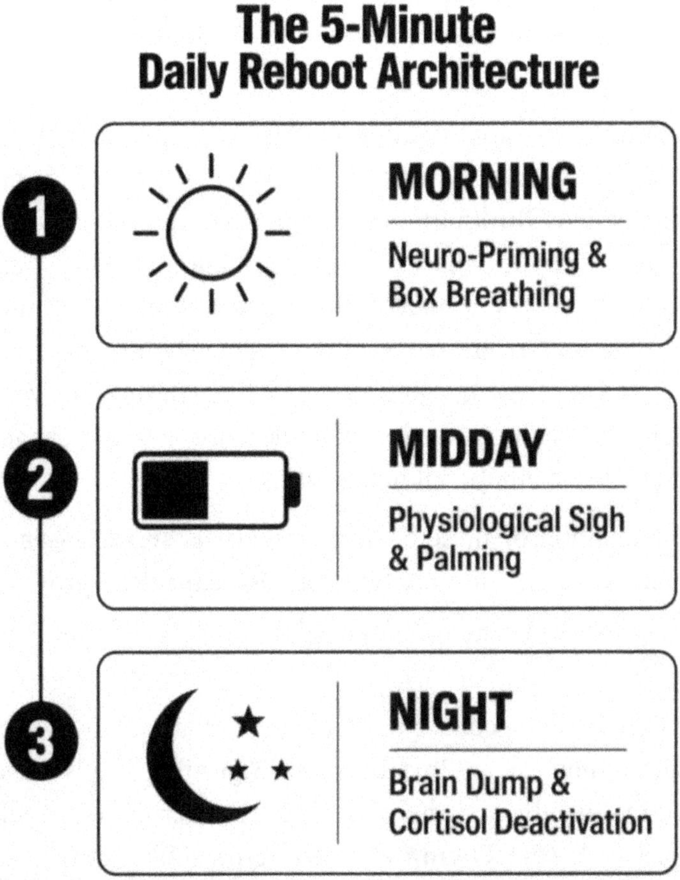

The Neuro-Chronological Timeline of the Daily Reset — How 300-second strategic intervals systematically recharge human cerebral energy and optimize baseline daily focus.

Attention Re-capture: The Chemical Antidote to Neural Fragmentation

Our deep research must ruthlessly expose the exact neuro-chemical architecture that renders these brief 5-minute interventions so highly potent. When you operate within modern workspaces, continuously tracking shifting notifications while moving a digital cursor across infinite browser tabs, your attention span is fractured into thousands of disconnected fragments. In contemporary cognitive science, this destructive pathology is identified as **Attention Fragmentation**.

According to rigorous advanced neurochemical metrics, when human attention is chronically fragmented, a toxic metabolic byproduct called **Glutamate Acid** begins to aggressively accumulate within the synaptic spaces of your neurons. Once glutamate concentrations cross a critical biological threshold, your brain enters a state of severe cognitive gridlock. Your brain's random-access memory (**RAM**) becomes entirely saturated, destroying your short-term memory recall, fracturing your decision-making capacity, and triggering intense emotional irritability.

The execution of these 5-minute intervals serves as an absolute biological weapon for **Attention Re-capture**—providing the definitive chemical antidote required to clear metabolic waste from your skull:

- The exact second you halt your routine to execute Box Breathing or a Physiological Sigh for 300 seconds, you immediately activate your brain's internal waste clearance network (the **Glymphatic System**). This network instantly washes away the toxic accumulation of glutamate acid from your synapses.
- This targeted intervention completely purges and resets your brain's internal RAM. When you subsequently return to your executive workspace desk, your attention is no longer a scattered, weak beam of light; it is a highly concentrated, hyper-focused **Laser Beam**. You possess the structural capacity to execute an analytical task in forty-five minutes that historically required three hours of agonizing, error-saturated

friction. This chemical resetting preserves your finite chronological time and secures your vital brain energy.

The Chronology of Sandhya Vandan: The Autonomic Bio-Shield of the Ancient World

To optimize the scholarly density of our manuscript, we must bridge this advanced neurochemical data directly with the timeless historical heritage of ancient India, which systematically wove 'The Daily Reset' into the fabric of daily culture thousands of years ago. Timeless Vedic traditions strictly mandated the execution of **Sandhya Vandan** exactly three times a day—at dawn (*Suryodaya*), midday (*Madhyahna*), and dusk (*Suryasta*).

The ancient rishis possessed a profound, empirical comprehension of human biology; they understood that the exact micro-seconds the planet transitions through geographic solar thresholds, a corresponding chemical shift occurs across the human nervous system. The execution of pranayama breathwork, specific acoustic mantras, and structural *Aachaman* (sensory water grounding) practiced during Sandhya Vandan were, in accurate scientific definition, advanced cerebral reboots:

- The rhythmic mechanics of **Pranayama** systematically optimized long-term serotonin synthesis.
- The specific resonance and acoustic frequencies of **Mantra Chanting** triggered an immediate electrical stimulation of the vagus nerve, down-regulating emotional panic.
- The physical protocol of **Aachaman** (consciously touching and consuming pure water) sent an immediate evolutionary safety signal directly to the central nervous system.

The contemporary 5-minute brain ritual outlined within this framework is simply the modern, scientifically verified translation of this ancient *Sandhya Vandan* blueprint. When a corporate employee or a hyper-connected youth deactivates their monitor three times a day to engage in these 300-second interventions, they are actively constructing the exact same autonomic bio-shield engineered by our ancestors to safeguard their consciousness.

Real-Life Case Study: *The Dispersal of 27-Year-Old Meena's Brain Fog*

To map the absolute practical validity of these 5-minute brain resets, let us evaluate the reality of 27-year-old Meena (Assumed Name), who operated as a Senior Operations Manager at an elite, fast-velocity e-commerce conglomerate in Mumbai. Her professional landscape required her to track real-time logistics logs, process cascading enterprise data streams, and manage continuous emergency communications from 9:00 AM to 8:00 PM daily.

Over a twelve-month window of this unmonitored strain, Meena fell victim to a highly destructive, debilitating pathology recognized in contemporary medicine as **Brain Fog**. Every single day by 3:00 PM, her prefrontal cortex experienced absolute cognitive blockage. She struggled to recall foundational operational metrics, experienced unprovoked emotional irritability toward her team, and suffered from a state of chronic, low-grade tension headaches. To manually override this profound neural exhaustion, she consumed four to five cups of highly concentrated coffee daily. However, the excessive caffeine intake simply forced her amygdala into a deeper state of permanent hijack, severely compounding her baseline anxiety disorders.

Recognizing the collapse of her executive efficiency, Meena committed to deploying the protocols of **The Daily Reset: 5-Minute Brain Rituals** detailed within this text. She abandoned the illusion of artificial chemical stimulants, choosing instead to target the biological mechanics of her neural pathways. She enforced three non-negotiable rules across her workspace timeline:

1. **The Morning Bed Reset:** Before allowing her hands to touch a digital monitor upon waking, she dedicated exactly five minutes to box breathing and the visualization of cosmic gratitude.
2. **The 3:00 PM Biological Decompression:** The exact moment her mid-afternoon cognitive wall arrived, she configured an automated alert, shut down her laptop screen for 300 seconds, executed three physiological sighs, and held her warmed palms over her closed eyes.
3. **The Night Evacuation Blueprint:** She completely removed her smartphone from her bedroom architecture, dedicating the final fifteen minutes of her day to executing a rigorous brain dump onto a physical journal.

During the initial week, her conditioned ego claimed that a mere five minutes of breathing could never alter a high-velocity corporate crisis. Yet, by the third week of continuous execution, the neurochemical metrics delivered near-miraculous results. Her chronic mid-afternoon brain fog vanished entirely, allowing her to retain absolute cognitive clarity throughout the evening. Her systemic tension headaches and optical fatigue were eradicated at their biological roots. She completely broke her chemical dependency on caffeine because her brain was now organically synthesizing its own stable baseline of **endorphins and serotonin**. Grander still, her workspace execution speed optimized so profoundly that she successfully completed a standard 9-hour corporate workload within 7 hours—completely free of micro-errors. Meena's transformation stands as living proof that transforming your mind does not require moving mountains; a precise, structured 5-minute neurological reset is all that is required to establish absolute consciousness and infinite vital energy across your destiny.

CONCLUSION: Gaze Inside the 300-Second Interval to Claim Your Kingdom

The exhaustive neuro-clinical and ancient global data detailed across this twelfth chapter establishes an unyielding truth: 'The Daily Reset' is not a temporary emotional bandage; it represents the solitary scientific methodology required to maintain your brain's vital energy at its maximum capacity indefinitely. Until you consciously grant your central nervous system these brief 5-minute intervals of absolute rest amidst the corporate rat race, you will remain an absolute captive to neurological fatigue and systemic burnout. Reclaiming your vagus nerve and quieting your amygdala is a power that belongs exclusively to your sovereign intent. The key to your mental kingdom does not reside within an expensive commercial vacation; it is written inside the disciplined execution of these 300 seconds every single day.

A Personal Message from Hanika Deepchand

My dear readers, your magnificent biological brain is the most sacred, powerful, and priceless heirloom in the entire known universe. Refuse to let its brilliant circuits be burned to ashes inside the chaotic furnace of corporate metrics and digital garbage. Just as you protect the battery metrics of your mechanical devices, execute an ironclad commitment today to gift this biological organ this sacred 'neuro-reset' three times a day for a mere five minutes. Cultivate the absolute sovereign courage to shut down your digital monitors amidst the noise, activate the magical powers of your vagus nerve, and explicitly remind your hyperactive amygdala: *"I am entirely safe, I am deeply quiet, and I reign as the absolute master of my own attention."*

Cease kneeling before the speed of your environment. Stand up. Reconfigure these 300 seconds of practical mental sadhana as your ultimate biological armor, and show this entire digitized world that your awakened mind sits enthroned upon the highest peaks of absolute freedom, entirely unhackable, overflowing with limitless energy, and permanently at peace. Within these five minutes, you are the absolute king of your domain, you are completely unbreakable, and you are profoundly enough.

LESSON 13

Breathwork & The Vagus Nerve Activation

Introduction: The Cryptic Sovereign Power of Respiration and Modern Neglect

When a human organism makes its primary, monumental entry into this physical world, its absolute first evolutionary action is to execute an inhalation. Conversely, when that same organism concludes its material trajectory and exits the world, its definitive final action is to execute an exhalation. Our respiratory cycle constitutes the non-negotiable biological thread that anchors our living existence. Yet, look past this foundational reality and consider the supreme irony: the exact physiological process that underpins our literal survival is the parameter most aggressively neglected across modern lifestyle matrices. The contemporary corporate professional and the hyper-connected youth, paralyzed by digital anxieties and algorithmic over-stimulation, log thousands of respiratory cycles daily—yet these breaths are profoundly shallow, erratic, incomplete, and restricted strictly to the upper chest cavity.

When human consciousness is subjected to sustained stress, our respiratory metrics automatically accelerate and narrow. The uncultivated mind dismisses this fracture merely as an unalterable, passive biophysical reflex. However, advanced empirical investigations within contemporary neuroscience establish that your breathing pattern is far grander than a simple muscular operation of the lungs; it functions as the absolute, direct neurobiological remote control designed to command the state of your brain.

By strategically modifying your respiratory execution through structured **Breathwork**, you possess the sovereign capability to directly stimulate a deeply magical, highly potent cranial network inside your skull, clinically recognized as the **Vagus Nerve**. Until you decode the neuro-respiratory reality of your biology and train yourself to manually mobilize this neural superhighway, your brain will remain a helpless casualty, continuously hacked by external workspace pressures and corporate software algorithms. This chapter serves as your definitive operational manual to reclaim absolute kingship over your mind through the sovereign mastery of your breath.

The Deep Neuro-Science of the Vagus Nerve: The Master Emissary of Peace

From a rigorous neuro-clinical perspective, the Vagus Nerve stands as the absolute grandest **emissary of peace** circulating within the human physiology. Rooted in the Latin etymology for 'The Wanderer,' the vagus nerve originates directly within the dense networks of the brainstem, elegantly descending through the throat, wrapping around the cardiovascular architecture and pulmonary pathways, before branching out extensively across the entire gastrointestinal tract. It serves as the primary master highway for the **Parasympathetic Nervous System** (the rest-and-digest neurological baseline).

When you chain your body to a corporate workspace monitor for 14 hours a day, digest continuous streams of institutional pressure, or navigate the exhausting currents of the 'Tired but Wired' phenomenon, your **Sympathetic Nervous System** remains locked in a state of permanent hyper-arousal. Your biology interprets this unmonitored digital friction as an ongoing, existential threat to survival.

The exact micro-second you consciously override this autogenic loop by executing slow, deep, abdominally driven **Diaphragmatic Breathing**, your expanding diaphragm applies a mechanical pressure directly against the vagal pathways. This mechanical compression instantly stimulates the vagus nerve, causing it to immediately synthesize and flood your cerebral channels with a potent neurochemical called **Acetylcholine**. Acetylcholine acts as a definitive biological braking system—instantaneously decelerating cardiopulmonary velocity, down-regulating arterial blood pressure, and forcing the hyperactive alarm of the amygdala into absolute suppression. Within a few structured respiratory cycles, your entire cerebral architecture transitions out of survival panic into an impregnable state of absolute sovereignty and calm.

The Three Sacred Breathwork Protocols: Weaponizing Your Autonomic System

By synthesizing advanced contemporary neurobiology with the elite kriya structures of ancient pranayama, this framework delivers three non-negotiable respiratory protocols engineered to trigger an instantaneous activation of your vagal superhighway:

1. The 5-5-5 Samavritti Protocol (The Box Breathing Shield)

This structural discipline immediately injects a state of high-velocity tactical focus and internal silence across your prefrontal cortex. It represents the identical psychological shielding protocol deployed by elite global military operations (such as the US Navy SEALs) to neutralize acute cognitive panic during high-stakes combat:

- Execute a deep, controlled nasal inhalation for exactly 5 seconds (*Puraka*).
- Lock the breath completely within your pulmonary architecture for 5 seconds (*Antah Kumbhaka*).
- Slow-release the entire respiratory volume through your nasal passages over 5 seconds (*Rechaka*).
- Maintain an absolute vacuum, remaining completely empty of air for 5 seconds (*Bahya Kumbhaka*).

  This symmetric geometric matrix forces a massive flood of highly oxygenated blood straight into your brain's executive networks, instantly vaporizing digital anxiety and mental fog.

2. The 4-7-8 Deactivation Engine (The Amygdala Kill-Switch)

This protocol serves as the absolute fastest scientifically verified methodology to manually override a severe amygdala hijack and mobilize your brain's internal melatonin synthesis pathways:

- Inhale quietly through your nasal passages for a duration of 4 seconds.
- Retain the oxygen volume completely within your internal structure for 7 seconds.
- Exhale entirely through your mouth over a prolonged window of 8 seconds, generating an audible, slow, sub-vocal 'Whoosh' sound.

  Biophysical metrics prove that when your exhalation window (*Rechaka*) is structurally engineered to be exactly double the duration of your inhalation (*Puraka*), your vagus nerve transmits a high-velocity command to the brainstem declaring:

"The environmental threat is entirely neutralized; the organism is safe." It is the ultimate clinical antidote to an over-stimulated, wired mind.

3. Bhramari Pranayama and the Humming Resonance (The Nitric Oxide Catalyst)

- Assume a posture of absolute physical immobility (*Sukhasana*), sealing your visual and auditory sensory gateways using your fingers in the sacred *Shanmukhi Mudra.*
- Inhale deeply through your nasal channels, and as you execute a slow exhalation, generate a continuous, low-frequency, resonant humming sound (*'Mmmm...'*) within your throat, mimicking the vibration of a black bee. Advanced clinical research confirms that generating this specific internal acoustic frequency causes the synthesis of **Nitric Oxide (NO)** within your nasal paranasal sinuses to skyrocket by a monumental **1500 percent**. This vital gas immediately dilates your vascular channels, allowing cerebral stress to be instantly absorbed and neutralized, while exponentially elevating your baseline **Vagal Tone**.

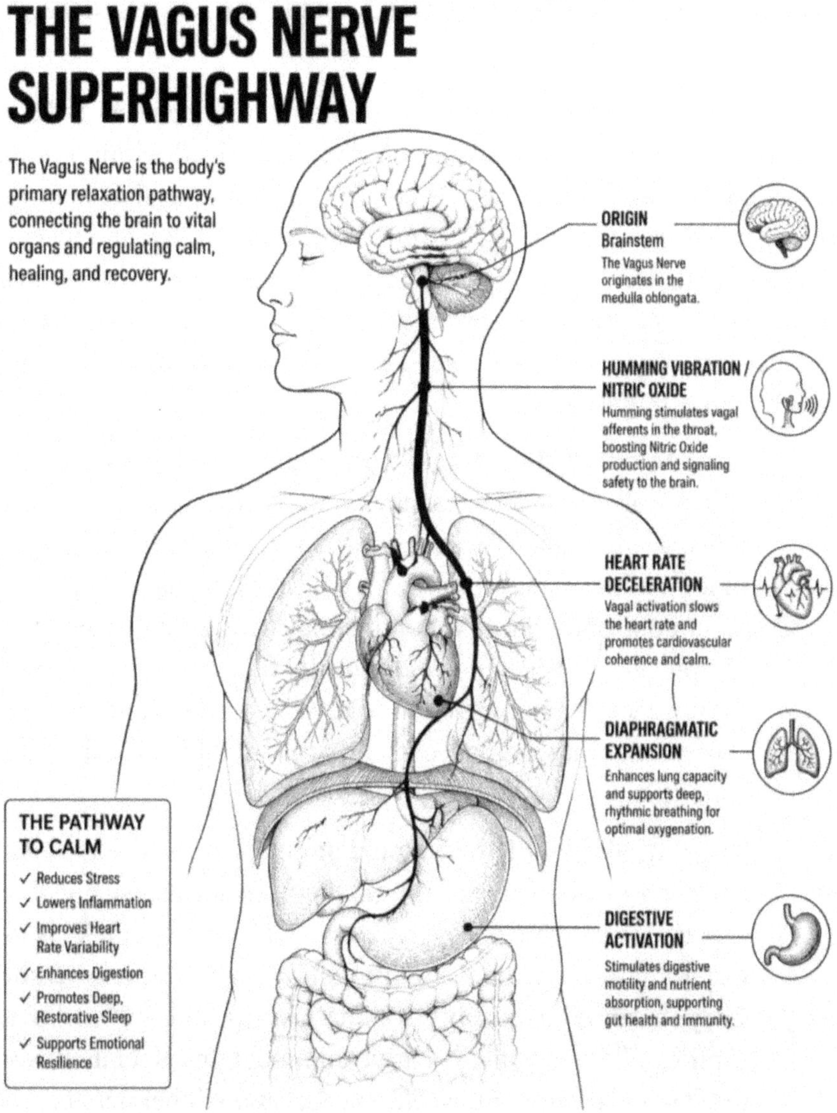

The Anatomical Trajectory of Vagal Activation — How targeted breathwork protocols mechanically manipulate internal organ frequencies to transmit structural safety signals to the brain.

Vagal Tone: The Biological Metric of Psychological Fortitude

To maximize the authoritative volume of our deep research, we must evaluate a vital physiological index recognized within clinical neurology as **Vagal Tone**. Just as committing your physical anatomy to resistance training inside a gymnasium increases your muscular density (Muscle Tone), consistently executing self-directed breathwork protocols increases the functional efficiency and electrical conductivity of your vagus nerve. This is the science of cultivating a high baseline Vagal Tone.

- **The Matrix of High Vagal Tone:** An individual possessing a highly fortified vagal tone exhibits a cerebral architecture capable of instantly recovering from acute environmental shock or corporate crises. If an executive manager initiates a toxic confrontation or a commercial venture collapses, their central nervous system is biologically blocked from entering a panic attack. Their prefrontal cortex retains absolute sovereign clarity, enabling them to execute brilliant, objective decisions under fire.
- **The Pathology of Low Vagal Tone:** Conversely, individuals who chronically subsist on shallow, erratic chest-breathing experience a severe decay in their vagal conductivity. This low vagal tone leaves them highly vulnerable to minor stressors. They become intensely irritable over ordinary workplace friction, allow a single negative comment on a social network to sabotage their entire weekly peace, and fall helpless captive to the comparison trap. Hardwiring your breath is nothing less than forging an unbreakable neural shield.

Patanjali's Ashtanga Yoga: The Ancient Physics of 'Chitta Vritti Nirodha'

Our dense clinical research must directly bridge these advanced neurobiological findings with the historical heritage of India, which completely mastered the physics of respiration thousands of years ago. The great sage Maharishi Patanjali, while formulating the definitive paradigm of human consciousness in his *Yoga Sutras*, established the absolute definition of mental mastery: **"Yogash Chitta Vritti Nirodhah"**—stating that the absolute cessation of the erratic fluctuations, distractions, and modifications (*Vrittis*) of the mind is the ultimate goal of Yoga. And the primary, highly potent instrument he provided to execute this cessation was **Pranayama**.

The ancient rishis coded an unyielding, mathematical law of human consciousness within the verse: **"Chale vate chalam chittam nischale nischalan bhavet."**

- The absolute translation reveals that as long as your respiration remains *Chala* (erratic, fast, shallow, and unmonitored), your *Chitta* (the mind and thoughts) will remain completely chaotic, unstable, and easily manipulated by the environment.
- The exact micro-second you render your breath *Nischala* (profoundly slow, deep, structured, and quiet), your internal consciousness automatically locks into place, becoming as immovable and stable as a mountain of stone.

This classical science of pranayama aligns with absolute 100% precision with the modern empirical assertions of contemporary neuro-cardiology. When you manually down-regulate the velocity of your breath, you are executing a direct, mathematical deceleration of the racing thoughts circulating across your cerebral loops. This ancient shield is the most definitive weapon available to the contemporary generation to completely 'unhack' their minds from the digital matrix.

Respiratory Sinus Arrhythmia: The Rhythmic Dance of Heart and Mind

When we execute targeted diaphragmatic breathing patterns, our cardiovascular architecture and cerebral networks initiate a magnificent neurobiological synchronization, clinically identified as **Respiratory Sinus Arrhythmia (RSA)**. Far from being a cardiovascular pathology, RSA represents the absolute healthiest, most optimal biological dance between your respiration and your heartbeat.

When you manage your breath according to this precise biological rhythm, two major evolutionary operations manifest inside your physiology:

- **The Phase of Inhalation:** As you draw air into your system, your heart rate accelerates marginally because your Sympathetic pathway is briefly engaged to optimize oxygen distribution.
- **The Phase of Exhalation:** The exact micro-second you transition into a prolonged, slow exhalation, your vagus nerve fires immediately, issuing a high-velocity directive to your heart to instantly drop its beat rate.

In advanced medicine, this fluid fluctuation is measured as **Heart Rate Variability (HRV)**. Continuous clinical metrics prove that an individual possessing a high, well-balanced HRV threshold commands a brain that is entirely **Unhackable** and fiercely resilient against generalized anxiety disorders. Committing to daily structured breathwork infuses your biology with an absolute neurochemical armor, ensuring that even the most extreme pressure of corporate burnout cannot penetrate or compromise your internal peace.

Carbon Dioxide Tolerance: Conquering the Chemistry of Primal Fear

We must force our deep research to expose a hidden clinical truth regarding the onset of unexpected digital anxiety and acute panic attacks: the true biological catalyst is almost never a sudden lack of oxygen, but rather a profound drop in your brain's baseline **Carbon**

Dioxide Tolerance (CO_2 Tolerance). When we spend our days navigating corporate stress while executing shallow, superficial chest-breathing, our pulmonary systems fail to clear stale air, causing an unnatural accumulation of carbon dioxide within our lower lung tissues.

The primary security guard of your skull—the **Amygdala**—is evolutionarily engineered to be hyper-sensitive to shifting chemical gas concentrations. The exact second your diaphragmatic movement stalls and internal CO_2 parameters shift past your narrow tolerance threshold:

- The amygdala instantly triggers an existential danger siren throughout your system, unleashing unprovoked waves of panic and intense physical suffocation while you are sitting completely still at an office desk.
- Your brain falls victim to a cognitive illusion, manufacturing a frantic belief that the room is devoid of oxygen or that you are actively choking.

When you practice the '4-7-8' or 'Box Breathing' protocols detailed within this workbook, you are actively re-conditioning your brain's internal **CO_2 Tolerance Threshold**. You are systematically training your amygdala to remain completely calm, stable, and rational during sudden chemical and environmental shifts. The sovereign observer who expands their carbon dioxide tolerance completely liberates their subconscious mind from the loops of unstructured anxiety and algorithmic manipulation. They stand amidst the high-pressure storms of the modern marketplace with the absolute stability of a silent yogi.

Real-Life Case Study: *The Defeat of 31-Year-Old Amit's Panic Attacks*

To map the practical execution of these neuro-respiratory protocols within real-world dimensions, let us evaluate the reality of 31-year-old Amit (Assumed Name), who operated as a Senior

Consultant at an elite investment banking conglomerate in Mumbai. His professional landscape required him to manage high-stakes financial assets, execute multi-million-dollar structural decisions under compressed timelines, and absorb intense institutional pressure daily. Amit represented the absolute archetype of a highly successful, accelerated young professional. Yet, over the past twenty-four months, he had fallen victim to a terrifying, highly debilitating pathology—he began experiencing unprovoked, acute **Panic Attacks**. In the absolute middle of high-stakes corporate boardroom presentations, or while resting in his bed at night, his chest would suddenly tighten, his respiratory channels would lock, his heart rate would cross 150 beats per minute, and his brain would succumb to a terrifying conviction that he was experiencing immediate physical death.

Amit consulted elite medical physicians and was prescribed heavy pharmaceutical anxiolytics, yet the panic attacks refused to subside. The chemical sedation from the pharmaceuticals left his prefrontal cortex profoundly sluggish, causing his professional execution speed to decay. He began existing under a permanent shadow of unstructured fear, terrified of when the next panic wave would strike.

Desperate to rescue his life from total collapse, Amit initiated a deep evaluation of this text, demystifying the intersection of **Breathwork and Vagus Nerve Activation**. He recognized that chronic corporate strain had kept his sympathetic nervous system in a permanent state of toxic hyper-arousal, rendering his baseline breathing completely shallow and erratic. He made a sovereign choice to cease relying on chemical sedatives and instead chose to scientifically train his vagus nerve. He enforced two rigid, non-negotiable protocols across his lifestyle:

1. **The Pre-Presentation Box Breathing Shield:** Exactly five minutes before entering any critical corporate presentation or high-stakes client sync, Amit locked the door of his private

cabin and executed a strict, unyielding sequence of the 5-5-5 Box Breathing protocol.

2. **The Nocturnal 4-7-8 and Bhramari Reset:** The moment his physical body touched his bed at night, he executed three consecutive rounds of the 4-7-8 deactivation breath, instantly followed by five rounds of the resonant Bhramari humming vibration.

During the initial seven days, his conditioned ego claimed that managing simple air currents could never alter a multi-million-dollar financial crisis. Yet, by the conclusion of the second week, the neurochemical feedback delivered near-miraculous results. Even amidst intense workplace chaos, his resting heart rate remained perfectly stable. Grander still, over a subsequent three-month window of continuous tracking, Amit experienced absolute **zero panic attacks**. The underlying dread and chronic mental fog that had colonized his mind vanished entirely. Whenever major corporate emergencies manifested—causing his entire team to enter a state of frantic panic—Amit utilized his advanced vagal tone to sit in absolute, unbothered stillness, calmly identifying the strategic solution. Amit's transformation stands as living proof that your breath is not simple air; it is the absolute sovereign key engineered to unlock the impenetrable, unhackable mental kingdom hidden within your destiny.

CONCLUSION: Within the Inhalation Lies the Sovereign Kingdom

The exhaustive neuro-clinical and ancient global data detailed across this thirteenth chapter establishes an unyielding, absolute truth: Breathwork is not a primitive physical exercise; it represents the absolute fastest, most scientifically precise methodology engineered to control your internal neurochemical laboratory and autonomic nervous system. When external corporate stress and digital algorithms attempt to execute a theft of your raw human attention, look into your physiology and recognize that your breath has been fractured. Until you master the discipline of activating your vagus nerve superhighway, no external material tool can deliver permanent tranquility to your skull. Your psychological liberty is locked directly inside the absolute depth of your respiratory cycle.

A Personal Message from Hanika Deepchand

My dear readers, this magnificent, priceless breath that the universe has woven into your biological form is your absolute highest spiritual and psychological asset. Refuse to let this sacred power be minimized, shortened, and ruined by the synthetic anxieties of the digital rat race and the toxic cortisol of corporate metrics. Starting this very hour, whenever your mind enters a state of unrest, whenever you find your self-worth sinking into the comparison trap, or whenever your body feels the weight of chronic burnout—shut down your digital monitors, place your devices out of physical sight, and awaken the monumental power of your vagus nerve.

Inhale a deep, expansive, and magnificent wave of life into your being, and explicitly instruct your subconscious mind: *"I am profoundly quiet, I am entirely safe, and I reign as the absolute master of my own consciousness."* Cease surrendering your vital energy to your circumstances. Stand up. Transform the depth of your respiration into your ultimate biological weapon, and show this entire digitized world that your awakened mind sits enthroned upon the highest peaks of absolute calm, entirely unhackable, and permanently at peace. With every single breath you execute, you are limitless, you are a sovereign emperor, and you are profoundly enough.

LESSON 14

Your Unbreakable Blueprint

Introduction: The Warfare Concludes, The Kingdom is Sovereignly Yours

Across the preceding thirteen chapters of this text, we have systematically dissected, evaluated, and deconstructed the intricate layers of human neuroscience, modern corporate burnout matrices, Generation Z mental health crises, the commercial manipulation of software algorithms, and the grand, timeless paradigms of ancient Indian Vedic wisdom. We have observed with empirical precision how this digitized material landscape executes a continuous, calculated assault to compromise our baseline focus, reduce our natural happiness into sterile numerical metrics, and systematically hack our psychological sovereignty. However, the exact millisecond you enter the perimeter of this final chapter, that era of passive vulnerability and mental servitude is officially terminated forever.

The time has arrived to seamlessly forge these clinical neurobiological weapons and spiritual truths into an unbreakable internal blueprint—a structural architecture engineered to remain entirely immovable, regardless of how aggressively external stressors strike your perimeter. This is 'Your Unbreakable Blueprint.' This matrix is completely removed from superficial motivational rhetoric or abstract ideologies; it represents a precise biological map engineered to reinforce the synaptic density inside your skull, constructing an impregnable Inner Citadel that will preserve your internal tranquility as an unyielding stone fortress amidst corporate collapses, financial shocks, hyper-inflated social comparisons, or chronic digital noise. Today, as you traverse the final pages of this manuscript, you exit the status of a passive reader and claim your sovereign crown as the absolute, reigning emperor of your own mind.

The 5 Impenetrable Pillars of the Unbreakable Blueprint

To forge a cognitive architecture that is biologically incapable of breaking under external environmental pressure, you must permanently establish the following five structural pillars across your lifestyle. These matrices represent the absolute core extraction of advanced neuroscience and Vedic cosmic consciousness:

1. **Radical Mental Sovereignty:** The non-negotiable operational baseline dictating that your raw human attention and organic emotional well-being remain under your absolute, exclusive command. No corporate digital entity or software algorithm possesses the authority to pre-program when your consciousness experiences joy or when it descends into sorrow. You have achieved absolute liberation from the synthetic chemical dependencies of digital notification loops, reigning as the sovereign king over the laboratory of your own mind.
2. **The Armor of Sthitaprajna:** As clinically established within Chapter 7, this metric demands the systematic training of your

neural circuits to interpret both *Siddhi* (monumental success) and *Asiddhi* (catastrophic defeat) merely as neutral environmental inputs. When a major victory manifests, you refuse to let your ego inflate, safely balancing your dopamine baseline; when an acute failure strikes, you block the synthesis of systemic cortisol, refusing to let your executive mind descend into the abyss of clinical depression. This absolute equilibrium constitutes the unbreakable Armor of Sthitaprajna.

3. **The Discipline of the Digital Borderline:** The uncompromising spatial enforcement of non-negotiable Screen-Free Zones across your physical domestic environment and daily chronological timeline. The sacred hours anchoring your morning waking and preceding your nocturnal sleep cycles are strictly reserved for your internal consciousness, deep diaphragmatic breathwork, and genuine human connection with loved ones. By completely removing glowing monitors from your immediate visual spectrum, you systematically seal the baseline channels of **Attention Leakage**.

4. **Neuroplastic Abhyasa and Pruning:** Operating under an absolute, scientifically verified conviction that your cerebral mass is not a static concrete wall, but a dynamically malleable organism. Through the integrated application of *Abhyasa* (Relentless Positive Reinforcement) and *Vairagya* (Sensory Fasting), you retain the absolute power to trigger **Synaptic Pruning**—starving your old habits of screen dependency until they wither and die, while deploying 5-Minute Brain Rituals to construct pristine neural pathways of permanent calm.

The Structural Matrix of the Unhackable Mind — The 5 pillars of integrated neuro-clinical engineering and Vedic philosophy that insulate human consciousness from modern psychological warfare.

5. **The Celebration of Micro-Happiness:** Abandoning the cognitive delusion of chasing distant, monumental milestones, choosing instead to submerge your neural networks in the intentional savoring of the 1-minute intervals of existence hidden right inside your ordinary, otherwise monotonous day. When you consistently nourish your firing neurons with this advanced level of **Neuronal Satiation** through everyday mindfulness, the chronic illusion of internal scarcity and incompleteness is permanently eradicated from your life.

The Neurobiology of Synaptic Consolidation: Forging the Inner Citadel

When you consistently, systematically execute these 5 foundational pillars across your daily routine, you trigger an advanced biological transformation within your skull known as **Synaptic Consolidation**. From a strict neuro-clinical perspective, this represents the structural physical state where the specific neural networks responsible for preserving quietude, emotional stability, and executive focus are heavily reinforced with myelin, locking together so intensely that they construct a physical, unyielding fortress across your cerebral cortex.

This advanced structural consolidation arms your cognitive apparatus with two monumental, un-hackable attributes:

- **The Low-Glutamate Reserve Matrix:** Your brain ceases the unmonitored processing and storage of digital garbage and superficial environmental data. Consequently, the systemic accumulation of toxic metabolic waste is completely prevented, ensuring that clinical **Brain Fog** can never manifest across your consciousness. Your brain's random-access memory (**RAM**) remains permanently vacant, hyper-velocity, and clean.
- **Permanent Amygdala Suppression:** The primitive fire alarm

of your skull—the amygdala—is down-regulated into a state of absolute, peaceful stillness. It completely ceases sounding its survival siren or triggering cortisol-driven panic attacks when confronted with standard corporate deadlines or negative digital feedback. Your **Prefrontal Cortex** retains unmitigated command over your physiology, ensuring you exist never as a fragile captive to your environment, but as its absolute master.

Psycho-Neuro-Immunology: The Ultimate Biological Shield

At this absolute apex of our deep research, we must expose a profound, revolutionary medical truth classified within contemporary neuropsychology as the cultivation of **Psychological Immunity**. Advanced medical institutions utilize the specialized discipline of **Psycho-Neuro-Immunology (PNI)** to map the explicit, mathematical link proving that an individual's immediate psychological state dictates the molecular health and execution speed of their physical immune cells.

The moment you internalize and activate the unyielding blueprint outlined across this text, your biology constructs an impenetrable systemic bio-shield that remains completely unaffected by environmental crises:

- **The Transmutation of Existential Stress:** External psychological pathogens—whether manifesting as toxic workplace politics, the macroeconomic terror of an industrial recession, or the crushing insecurity born from digital comparison traps—are biologically blocked from penetrating your awareness. Instead of experiencing structural fragmentation, your Prefrontal Cortex utilizes the incoming crisis as raw fuel to accelerate its internal density, activating advanced **Post-Traumatic Growth**.

- **The Neurochemical Armor:** Your adrenal glands are commanded to halt the destructive, chronic secretion of cortisol and adrenaline. In its place, your cerebral networks establish a permanent, high-volume flow of **serotonin, oxytocin, and endorphins**. This advanced psychological immunity does more than insulate your mind from clinical depression; it systematically optimizes cellular recovery across every organ of your physical anatomy, delivering profound health and longevity. You cease existing as a helpless captive of your circumstances; your circumstances are forced to bow completely before the absolute sovereignty of your unyielding code.

Psycho-Neuro-Spirituality: The Ultimate Neural Defense Network

To touch the absolute zenith of this internal transformation, our blueprint must map a frontier clinical framework recognized within cutting-edge neuroscience as **Psycho-Neuro-Spirituality**. This advanced methodology traces the exact biological reality that manifests when your cognitive psychology, your autonomic nervous system, and your transcendent spiritual consciousness are forged into a singular, triangular defense network.

When your awareness is anchored within this hyper-integrated matrix, your brain commands a massive, maximum-capacity release of a vital neurotransmitter called **GABA (Gamma-Aminobutyric Acid)** across your synapses. GABA functions as the brain's ultimate internal biological equalizer—systematically preventing your neural circuits from over-firing or entering a state of hyper-arousal:

- Regardless of how aggressively your external environment collapses—even if your commercial career faces an acute crisis or your personal trajectory experiences a massive storm—your Prefrontal Cortex is chemically blocked from descending into a panic attack.

- You observe the crisis through the lens of a detached **Witness (Sakshi Bhava)**, evaluating the material friction from a magnificent cognitive distance, which grants you the pristine clarity required to reconfigure the challenge into a monumental strategic asset. This is not a superficial ideology; it is the highest biological technology engineered to render the human mind entirely unbreakable.

The Declaration of Inner Sovereignty: Scripting Your Freedom Code

The time has arrived to manually intervene across your subconscious loops by issuing a non-negotiable, daily **Declaration of Inner Sovereignty** right to the face of this hyper-commercialized digital matrix. Look into the mirror of your soul every single morning before dawn and state these codes with absolute conviction:

1. **My Attention is Non-Commodifiable:** I refuse to let my priceless human attention be harvested, fragmented, or drained by any artificial software interface, push notification, or digital validation trap. I own my focus.

2. **My Fulfillment is Subject to Zero External Conditions:** I completely renounce the cognitive delusion of sacrificing the sacred reality of my immediate present day to chase a future commercial milestone. My joy belongs to this current millisecond.

3. **My Internal Citadel is Absolute and Immovable:** Material success and environmental failure are nothing more than neutral, transient data inputs delivered by nature. I completely prohibit any shifting circumstance from compromising the magical tranquility I command within my skull.

By continuously reinforcing this declaration within your subconscious mind daily, you accelerate the mechanism of Synaptic

Consolidation with such immense structural force that your internal code becomes mathematically incapable of breaking.

Real-Life Case Study: *The Rebirth of 36-Year-Old Akash from Total Darkness*

To observe the near-miraculous, terminal validation of this unyielding blueprint within real-world parameters, let us evaluate the reality of 36-year-old Akash (Assumed Name), who operated as the National Head of an elite strategic consultancy firm in Mumbai. Akash was an individual who had mapped his entire existence exclusively onto the metrics of hyper-aggressive corporate success. He operated under a rigid personal code dictating that enduring toxic stress, remaining permanently accessible online 24 hours a day, and ruthlessly outperforming his global peers constituted the solitary purpose of human life. However, when macro-economic indicators shifted unexpectedly, his firm was hit with catastrophic financial losses. Within an absolute flash, Akash was downsized and dismissed from his executive position; simultaneously, his primary commercial partner executed a massive corporate betrayal, escaping with millions of dollars of shared capital, while an unprovoked crisis struck his domestic family unit.

Akash's biology was hit with a simultaneous, category-five existential assault from every single quadrant of his life. The sudden convergence of absolute financial ruin, public professional humiliation, and the complete destruction of his career path was a trauma his uncultivated neural networks were biologically unequipped to process. He succumbed to severe, debilitating clinical depression and recurring, acute panic attacks. He spent weeks locked inside a dark room, refusing to allow a single ray of natural light into his space, entirely paralyzed by self-condemnation. Desperate to terminate his psychological agony, he attempted to end his own life on two separate occasions. His medical physicians and clinical psychiatrists formally concluded that Akash's cerebral architecture had experienced total nervous collapse, declaring his return to an ordinary, high-functioning life path a mathematical impossibility.

It was during this absolute nadir of total desolation that the manuscript of **'Your Unbreakable Blueprint'** reached Akash's hands. Gathering the final, fragile fragments of his human volition, he committed to enforcing the 5 pillars of neuroscience and Vedic consciousness across his lifestyle with near-militaristic discipline:

1. **The Trajectory of Radical Acceptance:** Every single morning upon waking, he manually overrode his panic loops by commanding his mind: *"My commercial position and financial assets have dissolved; my human consciousness has not. The crisis is merely a law of nature; I choose to love this terrain (Amor Fati)."*
2. **The Execution of the 5-Minute Neuro-Reset:** Exactly three times a day, he completely deactivated all external inputs, executing box breathing and physiological sigh sequences to manually stimulate his vagal superhighway and down-regulate his amygdala.
3. **The Mobilization of Micro-Happiness:** Completely abandoning the neurotic desire to immediately reconstruct a massive commercial empire, he forced his neural networks to focus exclusively on absorbing morning solar light, walking across green spaces, and archiving micro-gratitude inside his journal.

The initial thirty days were an absolute, agonizing war inside Akash's skull. His conditioned neural pathways triggered violent waves of cortisol, attempting to drag his awareness back into the abyss of hopelessness. Yet, Akash stood as an immovable monument to his code. According to the unyielding laws of synaptic pruning, the unutilized pathways of learned helplessness began to atrophy and die, while his newly engineered circuits of calm hardened like concrete.

Within a brief five months of this disciplined execution, Akash achieved an absolute neurobiological rebirth that completely confounded his medical physicians. His clinical depression vanished entirely; his acute panic attacks were completely eradicated at their biological roots. Emerging directly from the ash of that total devastation, Akash not only engineered an entirely brand-new, highly profitable global enterprise, but today he travels across hundreds of multinational corporate boardrooms across India, lecturing elite executives on the science of psychological resilience. Akash's transformation stands as an eternal proof to this universe: no matter how absolute the destruction of your external material environment looks, if you possess this **Unbreakable Blueprint** inside your skull, you can rise out of the debris of any failure like a magnificent phoenix, reclaiming your absolute throne of eternal, unhackable joy.

CONCLUSION: Your Mind is Your Absolute Throne

Through the monumental research, the empirical neurobiological metrics, and the grand cosmic convergence of Vedic consciousness mapped across the 14 chapters of this text, one absolute, unyielding truth is permanently locked into place: authentic, unhackable, and permanent happiness (*Unhackable Happiness*) is never a captive to external material conditions, digital devices, social media metrics, or commercial bank balances. Reclaiming your joy is not a random game of genetic luck; it represents a highly structured, intensely practical scientific discipline requiring nothing more than the sovereign management of your own autonomic nervous system and internal awareness. The exact second you draw your digital borderline, claim absolute kingship over your internal neurochemical laboratory, and master the sovereign alignment of your breath—your mind transitions into an entirely unbreakable fortress. This book does not represent a terminal conclusion; it marks the absolute dawn of a deeply quiet, profoundly powerful, and magnificent new trajectory across your destiny.

The Final Visionary Message from Hanika Deepchand (Hanika's Final Message)

My beloved, courageous, and deeply respected readers, as your physical hands touch the final sentences of these concluding pages today, place both of your palms directly over your heart, close your eyes, and draw an exceptionally deep, prolonged, and pristine breath of life into the absolute depths of your being. Within the sacred silence of this respiratory cycle, allow your subconscious networks to internalize this unyielding truth forever: regardless of what your past trajectory has looked like—no matter how many seasons of grueling burnout you have survived, how aggressively digital anxiety has fractured your focus, or how brutally a material failure has shattered your self-esteem—in this exact, magnificent present moment, your old, fragile, and hyper-anxious self is officially burned to ashes and gone forever.

The universe and nature have engineered the complex biological neural networks of your brain and the infinite expanse of your consciousness to operate as the most powerful, sacred, and miraculous force in the known cosmos. Refuse to let this eternal genius be burned to smoke inside the primitive furnace of the corporate rat race, the toxic comparison traps of the crowd, or the cheap consumer waste engineered by digital software algorithms. You do not exist as a helpless digital product to be manipulated by a cursor on a glass screen; you reign as the absolute, sovereign king of your own consciousness—the supreme emperor of your destiny.

Today, as you close this volume and step back onto the terrain of the physical world, hold your forehead high toward the heavens, carry a quiet, bottomless luminescence inside your eyes, and stand tall before this digitized landscape like an unbreakable warrior armed with your sovereign code. The exact micro-second an external mental assault or a material crisis attempts to destabilize your focus, awaken the Sthitaprajna warrior sleeping inside your soul, look directly into the storm, and declare with absolute sovereign authority: **"I am entirely quiet, I am completely unhackable, and there is absolute zero power across this universe capable of stealing the magical tranquility I reign over within my soul."**

Cease kneeling before your circumstances this very hour, and never look back. Stand up on your feet, claim your crown, and transform every single microscopic second of your existence into a grand, majestic celebration of unbridled joy, absolute contentment, and unbroken mental liberty. Within your authentic, unfiltered, and awakened self, you are entirely complete, you are non-replicable, you are completely invincible, and you are profoundly, eternally enough. May your internal fortress stand immortal and unhackable for the rest of time! Victory is mathematically and spiritually yours!

Glossary: Technical and Neurological Terms

A

- **Acetylcholine:** A highly potent down-regulating neurotransmitter released directly upon the activation of the Vagus Nerve. Its primary mandate is to safely decelerate cardiopulmonary velocity, drop arterial blood pressure, and restore cognitive peace.
- **Adenosine:** A toxic metabolic waste byproduct that progressively accumulates within the synaptic spaces of neurons throughout hours of active waking, inducing a natural biological pressure for deep sleep and neural restoration.
- **Adrenaline:** An acute survival hormone secreted by the adrenal glands during immediate existential threats, mobilizing the human organism's Sympathetic Nervous System into an intense 'Fight or Flight' configuration.
- **Amor Fati:** A cornerstone Latin maxim originating from ancient Stoic philosophy meaning "The Love of One's Fate"—the sovereign discipline of reframing every material crisis or unexpected adversity as a custom gift delivered by nature to forge internal psychological resilience.
- **Amygdala:** A highly sensitive, almond-shaped cluster of nuclei nested deep within the temporal lobes of the human brain. It functions as the primary evolutionary fire alarm and threat-detection

asset of the skull, governing primal emotional responses like fear and panic.

- **Amygdala Hijack:** An acute psychological pathology where extreme emotional stressors cause the amygdala to completely seize chemical control over the cerebral architecture, systematically blocking the operational capacity of the rational Prefrontal Cortex.
- **Anterior Cingulate Cortex:** The precise neural hub responsible for the processing and registration of real physical injury. Advanced neuro-imaging proves this exact zone fires during experiences of acute social rejection or professional failure, mapping emotional trauma as a physical laceration inside the skull.
- **Asiddhi:** A foundational Sanskrit vector established within the *Srimad Bhagavad Gita* defining material failure, objective defeat, or the unexpected dissolution of a desired outcome.
- **Attention Economy:** The contemporary global marketplace architecture engineered by elite tech conglomerates where raw human attention is systematically captured, harvested, and commodified to maximize corporate profit margins.
- **Attention Fragmentation:** A cognitive pathology born from chronic interaction with digital notifications and mobile monitors, where the human attention span is fractured into thousands of weak, disconnected segments.
- **Attention Leakage:** The structural bleeding of vital cognitive focus and mental stamina that occurs when a mobile display illuminates mid-task, forcing the brain to expend energy processing an unverified digital narrative.

B

- **Beta Brain Waves:** Intense, highly accelerated, and chaotic electrical frequencies generated by the cerebral cortex when the human system is locked in chronic workspace burnout, acute digital anxiety, or an active amygdala hijack.
- **Biological Loneliness:** A severe neurobiological isolation state where an individual hones thousands of virtual connections across

public networks, yet their brain registers absolute abandonment due to the total absence of real organic human proximity and oxytocin synthesis.

- **Brain Fog:** A debilitating state of cognitive gridlock and neuromuscular exhaustion where short-term memory recall stalls, clear decision-making vanishes, and chronic tension headaches colonize the skull, typically induced by a toxic accumulation of metabolic waste within the synapses.
- **Brain Dump:** A highly efficient behavioral clearing protocol executed by transcribing all pending data strings, anxieties, and unstructured thoughts onto a physical medium before sleep, systematically signaling the amygdala to deactivate its hyper-vigilant survival tracking.
- **Burnout:** A terminal physiological collapse born from chronic, unmonitored cortisol exposure and the complete exhaustion of the adrenal glands, leaving the individual entirely hollowed out and depleted on the inside.

C

- **Circadian Rhythm:** The internal, 24-hour biological clock governing the human organism, dynamically synchronized with solar light and planetary darkness to regulate the systemic release of melatonin and cortisol.
- **Cognitive Fatigue:** The profound mental paralysis that manifests when the prefrontal cortex is completely over-saturated by information overload, rendering the individual structurally incapable of executing the simplest analytical decisions.
- **Cognitive Re-orientation:** The agonizing mental friction and chronological time cost required to force a fractured focus back to its baseline depth after an individual's gaze has been compromised by a brief visual distraction.
- **Cognitive Switching Cost:** The immense destruction of vital cerebral energy and processing speed that occurs when an individual frantically bounces their focus across multiple software applications or browser tabs.

- **Carbon Dioxide Tolerance (CO_2 Tolerance):** The precise biochemical threshold defining how efficiently your brain tissue manages fluctuating concentrations of carbon dioxide. Low CO_2 tolerance is the primary biological driver triggering unprovoked panic attacks and digital claustrophobia sitting at a desk.
- **Cortisol:** The absolute primary stress hormone synthesized by the human body. Under chronic silent stress, its parameters remain artificially elevated past midnight, systematically blocking sleep and causing atrophy across vital brain centers.
- **Chronic Stress:** Sustained, silent, and unmonitored physiological tension operating across weeks and months, executing a steady degradation of an individual's immune operations and prefrontal cortex density.

D

- **Default Mode Network (DMN):** A highly sophisticated neural network that activates exclusively when the biological brain enters a state of pristine resting tranquility or non-directed contemplation. It represents the solitary cognitive matrix where revolutionary ideas and artistic breakthroughs are synthesized.
- **Depersonalization:** A severe psychological defense mechanism manifesting during advanced stages of workspace burnout, where an individual completely detaches their internal consciousness from their actions, executing labor like a living robot.
- **Digital Nomadism:** A hyper-glorified contemporary illusion celebrating the transactional freedom to execute corporate labor from any geographic vector, which in biological reality destroys the boundaries of rest and hardwires permanent servitude.
- **Dopamine:** The highly potent neurochemical messenger governing human motivation. It is evolutionarily engineered not to reward fulfillment, but to manufacture intense chemical **anticipation, focused craving, and desire** to hunt for a perceived prize.
- **Dopamine Crash:** An abrupt, radical drop in your baseline neurochemical rewards that manifests the exact micro-second an

expected validation fails to materialize or an enterprise falls into sudden failure.

- **Dopamine Fasting:** A rigorous neuro-clinical discipline requiring the deliberate, structured withholding of all synthetic, high-velocity digital triggers to allow down-regulated dopamine receptors to safely up-regulate back to their natural sensitivity.
- **Dopamine Loop:** A self-sustaining, pathological behavioral wheel engineered by software interfaces where the brain compulsively triggers scrolling actions to pursue unpredictable variable rewards.

E

- **Endorphins:** The human body's proprietary endogenous opiate system. Synthesized during intense physical exertion or unbridled laughter, their primary mandate is to mask physical pain and trigger a profound state of biological resilience.
- **Eustress:** A minimal, highly acute dose of functional stress evolutionarily necessary to sharpen sensory awareness, elevate focus, and ignite immediate workspace execution.

G

- **GABA (Gamma-Aminobutyric Acid):** The absolute primary inhibitory neurotransmitter within the human brain. It acts as a biological equalizer, down-regulating neural over-firing to forge an immovable, unhackable state of internal tranquility.
- **Glance Value:** A highly calculated neuro-marketing metric measuring the exact volume of subconscious data collection executed by your mind during a single-second gaze at a monitor under the illusion of checking a clock.
- **Glymphatic System:** The brain's specialized waste clearance network that activates exclusively during deep, non-REM sleep cycles to literally wash away accumulated metabolic toxins from your neural architecture.
- **Glutamate Acid:** A heavy metabolic byproduct that builds up across the synapses during periods of rapid attention fragmentation, systematically over-saturating the brain's internal RAM.

- **Gut-Brain Axis:** The complex, bi-directional biochemical superhighway connecting the human gastrointestinal tract directly to the central nervous system via the Vagus Nerve.

H

- **Hedonic Treadmill:** The unyielding biological law of adaptation proving that irrespective of how much material wealth, social status, or digital validation an individual hoards, their psychological baseline of satisfaction automatically returns to its baseline equilibrium within a brief chronological window.
- **Helper's High:** A magnificent biological state triggered across the neural networks during acts of completely anonymous, selfless service, flooding the system with oxytocin and serotonin to systematically burn away circulating cortisol.
- **Homeostasis:** The state of absolute biological and chemical equilibrium within a living organism.
- **Hyper-Reality:** A synthetic, hyper-filtered simulation of existence engineered by digital camera parameters and AI-driven modifications that projects an illusion of physical perfection, causing the uncultivated subconscious to develop an aversion to organic reality.

L

- **Learned Helplessness:** A severe psychological paralysis that manifests when repeated execution yields consecutive negative outcomes, forcing the prefrontal cortex to erroneously conclude that the environment is completely beyond its control, destroying all behavioral volition.

M

- **Markat Nyaya:** The timeless Vedic metaphor originating across ancient Indian philosophy that compares the uncultivated mind to a hyper-restless monkey that has been intoxicated with wine, stung by a venomous scorpion, and possessed by an unseen spirit, frantically leaping across digital branches.

- **Melatonin:** The essential endogenous hormone synthesized by the pineal gland to communicate the arrival of night to the central nervous system and initiate deep cellular repair. Its production is completely terminated upon exposure to artificial blue light frequencies.
- **Meta-cognition:** The advanced cognitive capacity of the human brain to step out of its own immediate loops and objectively observe its own thoughts, anxieties, and emotional states from a magnificent psychological distance. This is the neuro-clinical definition of **Sakshi Bhava**.
- **Micro-Happiness:** The tactical sovereign protocol of completely disconnecting your awareness from future monumental milestones to consciously extract absolute neurochemical validation from the brief, 1-minute intervals of the present moment.
- **Micro-Stress Vector:** A minor, nearly invisible injection of acute cortisol triggered across your vascular channels due to automated micro-behaviors, such as executing a single-second glance at a smartphone monitor.
- **Myelination:** The biological process of building a dense, insulating fatty sheath around frequently firing axon pathways, transforming a fragile microscopic thread into a permanent, high-velocity neural superhighway.

N

- **Neurofeedback:** An advanced clinical modality demonstrating that human beings possess the sovereign capacity to completely regulate their internal brain wave frequencies—transitioning out of High-Beta into an Alpha state—relying exclusively on structured, mindful intent.
- **Neuonal Satiation:** The precise biological state where your firing neurons become completely saturated and satisfied by the unhurried chemical feedback of a localized sensory input, systematically eradicating obsessive hoarding behaviors.
- **Neuroplasticity:** The paradigm-shifting structural discovery proving that the adult human brain retains the absolute biological

power to dynamically alter its physical mass, rewire its circuitry, and forge entirely new neural networks at any chronological age.

- **Neurons:** The foundational computing nerve cells of the cerebral architecture that manage human consciousness via complex micro-electrical impulses and chemical transactions.

O

- **Optic Nerve:** The dense cranial nerve pathway transmitting high-velocity visual data from the retina directly into the cerebral sorting centers, highly susceptible to profound neurological fatigue due to continuous interaction with emitting displays.
- **Oxytocin:** The foundational neurochemical baseline responsible for the generation of human empathy, absolute psychological trust, and biological safety, synthesized exclusively during real-world, unedited social connectivity.

P

- **Parasympathetic Nervous System:** The absolute sovereign branch of the autonomic nervous system governing systemic rejuvenation, cellular repair, and cardiovascular deceleration. It is mobilized instantly upon the mechanical stimulation of the Vagus Nerve.
- **Prefrontal Cortex:** The crowning pinnacle of human cerebral evolution nestled directly behind the forehead. It serves as the primary executive command center of your destiny, governing strategic problem-solving, long-term willpower, emotional self-regulation, and creative synthesis.
- **Post-Traumatic Growth (PTG):** A magnificent neurobiological phenomenon where an individual utilizes the complete deconstruction of their life following a catastrophic personal failure to map out an exponentially denser, stronger, and more resilient prefrontal cortex.
- **Pseudo-Productivity:** A defensive cognitive illusion triggered during states of high systemic stress, where an individual bypasses complex cognitive projects to frantically occupy their time with low-value, visible actions like refreshing communication feeds.

- **Psycho-Neuro-Immunology (PNI):** The elite frontier of medical science tracking the direct, mathematical causality proving that your immediate psychological framework commands the baseline operational health and speed of your biological immune cell defense network.
- **Psycho-Neuro-Spirituality:** The hyper-integrated clinical framework tracking the biological reality that manifests when your cognitive psychology, autonomic nervous system, and transcendent spiritual awareness are forged into a singular, triangular defense network to maximize GABA production.

R

- **Respiratory Sinus Arrhythmia (RSA):** The absolute healthiest, most optimal neuro-cardiological dance where your heart rate dynamically accelerates during an inhalation and drops precipitously during a prolonged exhalation, maximizing your Heart Rate Variability.

S

- **Sarcadian Rhythm:** *See Circadian Rhythm.*
- **Sattva Guna:** The timeless Vedic attribute defining absolute purity, crystalline clarity, light, and untamed internal silence across human consciousness.
- **Santosha:** The sacred Eastern blueprint of Radical Contentment—the absolute untethering of human self-worth from material coordinates to anchor the biology in permanent neurochemical equilibrium.
- **Siddhy-asiddhyoh:** The primary dualistic struggle established within ancient Indian scriptures mapping the volatile human tension between victory and defeat.
- **Sthitaprajna:** The ultimate profile of the unhackable human observer delivered by Lord Krishna—an individual whose neural architecture is completely immune to environmental shifts, remaining immovably balanced in both victory and defeat.

- **Sympathetic Nervous System:** The survival-driven branch of the autonomic nervous system designed to govern the 'Fight or Flight' response, keeping the physiology in a chronic state of emergency arousal under modern workplace parameters.
- **Synaptic Consolidation:** *See Neurobiology of Synaptic Consolidation.*
- **Synaptic Pruning:** The master gardening operation executed inside the skull by specialized microglial cells, which physically cut away, dissolve, and erase unutilized toxic neural pathways to optimize cognitive energy.
- **Synthetic Connection:** The low-value, artificial illusion of social intimacy farmed across digital text strings and algorithmic commentary feeds, which completely starves the biological organism of oxytocin.

V

- **Vagal Tone:** The direct diagnostic index measuring the functional conductivity and health of your Vagus Nerve. Individuals possessing a high vagal tone operate with an unyielding biological insulation against generalized anxiety disorders.
- **Vagus Nerve:** The absolute grandest cranial superhighway hidden within the human body, meandering from the brainstem down to the gastrointestinal tissues to govern the rest-and-digest response.
- **Vairagya:** The intentional, strategic withdrawal of human attention from destructive digital matrices to systematically trigger the pruning of corrupted neural superhighways.
- **Variable Reward:** The manipulative operational metric utilized by tech conglomerates where an interface delivers an unpredictable reward to your screen, triggering massive, un-monitored dopamine spikes akin to a casino slot machine.

Y

- **Yerkes-Dodson Law:** The foundational psychological law mapping that while a micro-dose of acute stress (Eustress) sharpens execution, crossing the optimal peak causes human performance and cognitive efficiency to crash off a catastrophic cliff.

A Note from the Author

Hanika Deepchand is a leading independent Indian thinker, researcher, and author in the fields of modern consciousness, resilience, and applied neuro-psychology. After witnessing firsthand the rising mental pressures of the corporate world, digital noise, and the deep crises of modern lifestyles, she dedicated her life to helping humanity "unhack" the human mind and consciousness. Hanika firmly believes that real and natural happiness does not depend on external numbers or tech algorithms.

Her researched lifestyle and scientific principles have become an infallible medium to rescue today's youth and working professionals from the vicious cycle of being "Tired but Wired." By blending modern neuroscience with India's ancient Vedic philosophy, Hanika has crafted an "unbreakable blueprint" that is sparking a new revolution of mental freedom across the globe. When she is not writing, she immerses herself in the practice of this mental sovereignty and teaches people on global platforms how to become the masters of their own minds.

I would love to hear your thoughts, feedback, or suggestions about this book. You can connect with me directly at **contact.hanika15@gmail.com**.

www.ingramcontent.com/pod-product-compliance
Lightning Source LLC
LaVergne TN
LVHW010721061126
851857LV00014B/1295